Accessing Complex Texts

- Annotate
- Collaborate
- Think About Text

can't sit here very long," said the Rat. "The cold is too awful for anything, and the sno
be too deep for us to wade through." He peered about him and considered. "Look her
on, "this is what occurs to me. There's a sort of dell down here in front of us, where
nd seems all hilly and humpy and hummocky". We'll make our way down into that, an
some sort of shelter." So once more they got on their f   wn into th
re they hunted about for a cave or some corner that w   on from the
and the whirling snow. They were investigating one of   he Rat had
hen suddenly the Mole tripped up and fell forward on his face with a   l. "O my le
. "O my poor shin!" and he sat up on the snow and nursed his leg in both his front pa
r old Mole!" said the Rat kindly. You don't seem to be having much luck today, do you
a look at the leg. Yes, you've cut your shin, sure enough. Wait till I get at my handke
I'll tie it up for you." "I must have tripped over a hidden branch or a stump," said the
e   s a very clean cut," said the Rat, examining it again attentively. "That was n

Douglas Fisher • Nancy Frey

Table of Contents

61

145

5

89

Unit 1

Be Yourself

Table of Contents

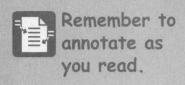
Notes

Narcissa

by Gwendolyn Brooks

1 Some of the girls are playing jacks.
Some are playing ball.
But small Narcissa is not playing
Anything at all.

5 Small Narcissa sits upon
A brick in her back yard
And looks at tiger-lilies,
And shakes her pigtails hard.

First she is an ancient queen
10 In pomp and purple veil.
Soon she is a singing wind.
And, next, a nightingale.

How fun to be Narcissa,
A-changing like all that!
15 While sitting still, as still, as still
As anyone ever sat!

Notes

Close Reading and Collaborative Conversations

What Does the Text Say?	How Does the Text Work?
1. What is this poem describing? Turn to a partner and summarize "Narcissa."	**1.** What is the narrator's point of view in this poem? How would the poem be different if it were from Narcissa's point of view?
2. What is the setting of this poem? Use evidence from the poem in your answer.	**2.** What image does the poet create in the first stanza? How does she build on it in the next stanzas?
3. Reread the first stanza. What is the poet comparing Narcissa to?	**3.** Reread the fourth stanza. What purpose do the exclamation marks have? How do they convey the author's point of view?

What Does the Text Mean?

1. What do you learn about Narcissa as a character from what she imagines herself to be?

2. How is this poem similar or different to other poems that you have read?

3. Is it better to play jacks and ball, or to sit and imagine? Explain which point of view the poem supports, or if it holds both activities of equal value.

Write About the Text

Opinion/Argument Writing Prompt

Do you think what Narcissa is doing is better or worse than playing ball or jacks? Write an essay defending your opinion. Support your discussion with evidence from the text.

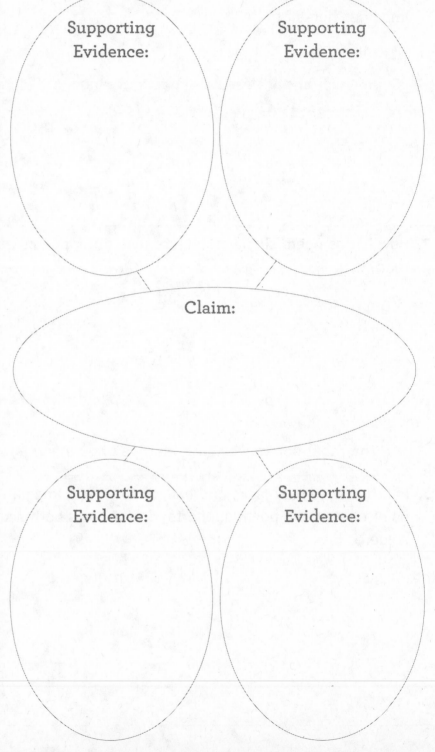

Plan your response using this graphic organizer. Use your annotations and your notes on pages 6–9 to find evidence for your essay.

Supporting Evidence:

Supporting Evidence:

Claim:

Supporting Evidence:

Supporting Evidence:

Writer's Checklist

- ❏ I introduced the topic and clearly stated my opinion.
- ❏ I grouped related ideas together.
- ❏ I used facts to support my opinion.
- ❏ I used linking words, including **for example**, **because**, and **in addition**, to connect my ideas.
- ❏ I have a concluding statement.

# Wrap Up
Check Your Understanding

1. This question has two parts. Answer Part A, then answer Part B.

   Part A In the first two stanzas, how does the author want the reader to feel about Narcissa?

   A. jealous of her because she is able to imagine many things

   B. sorry for her because she is not playing with the other girls

   C. worried for her because she is frightened of the other girls

   D. indifferent to her because she is hiding in her yard instead of playing

   Part B How do the last two stanzas influence the reader's opinion about Narcissa?

   A. They show that Narcissa is truly bored and can't even get up from her brick.

   B. They show that Narcissa would be happier if she played with the other girls.

   C. They show that Narcissa is secretly a queen.

   D. They show that Narcissa's imaginative play by herself is more fun than anything else.

2. What effect does repeating the word <u>still</u> in the last stanza have on the meaning of the poem?

   A. The repetition makes sure that we understand how bored Narcissa is.

   B. The repetition emphasizes how very quietly Narcissa was sitting.

   C. The repetition shows that Narcissa refuses to leave her garden and is still there.

   D. The repetition emphasizes the rhythmic way that Narcissa is moving.

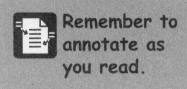
Notes

The Not-So-Ugly Duckling

1   On a warm sunny day, a duck sat upon her nest and waited for her eggs to hatch. The tiny ducklings crept from their eggs. One very large egg, however, had not yet burst. An old duck came by, examined the remaining egg, and said to Mother Duck, "That must be a turkey's egg. Turkeys are afraid of the water."

2   At the crack of dawn the great egg burst open and a large gray something or other crawled out of his shell. Mother Duck looked at him and wondered if he really could be a turkey chick, so she took him to the pond to see if he could swim. Sure enough, he plunged into the water.

3   Mother Duck took her flock to a poultry farm to live.

4   "Look at that ugly creature!" remarked a chicken.

5   And with that, the chicken approached Duckling and bit him on the neck.

6   Duckling was beaten and pushed by the ducks and the chickens. Even his brothers and sisters picked on him. The poor thing was scoffed at by the whole yard.

7   Duckling flew over a fence and through a meadow. He found a spot near a single tree and remained there, determined to lead a solitary life. In the afternoons, he'd dash into the water to swim and dive. But none of the creatures that he saw on his way greeted him.

Notes

8   Autumn came and the leaves in the forest turned yellow and brown. The winds were strong. The poor duckling ached with loneliness.

9   One evening just as the sun was setting, a flock of white birds with long, flexible necks appeared. They were swans. They uttered strange cries, opened their glorious wings, and flew away to warm lands. The ugly duckling watched them. He would never forget those beautiful birds. Duckling didn't know what they were, but he loved them more than any creature he had ever seen.

10   It would really be too sad to talk about all the miserable days and nights that Duckling had to endure during that first winter. He lay alone, stiff in the frost, for months.

11   At last the spring came and the sun melted the frost and warmed the air. Duckling flapped his wings, flew to the water, and plunged in. Then, from out of the thicket, came three glorious swans. Duckling remembered the lovely birds.

12   "I don't expect them to be my friends. But I will swim to them to see how they look up close on the water. Maybe when they see me, they will laugh at me because I am so ugly, but I don't care," cried Duckling. And he swam to the swans. They came toward him with outspread wings.

13   But what did he see in the clear water? He saw his own image. And he was no longer an ugly clumsy dark gray bird—but a beautiful swan with dazzling wings.

14   Somehow all the pain that he had known didn't matter. He was so happy now in the splendor that surrounded him. And the great swans swam around him and stroked him with their beaks.

Close Reading and Collaborative Conversations

What Does the Text Say?	How Does the Text Work?
1. What is this story mostly about? Turn to a partner and summarize "The Not-So-Ugly Duckling."	**1.** Does the first paragraph help the reader understand how sad the story will be? Why do you think the writer chose to begin the story this way?
2. Is Duckling happy or sad once he leaves the poultry farm to live under a tree? Use evidence to explain your answer.	**2.** What is the tone in paragraphs 7–10? What language does the author use to establish the tone?
3. Are the swans that Duckling meets at the end of the story kind or cruel to him? Explain your answer using evidence.	**3.** Why does the author save the information that Duckling is really a swan for the last few paragraphs of the story?

What Does the Text Mean?

1. Why were the animals cruel to Duckling? Were they justified in their treatment of him?

2. Was it important for the resolution of the story that Duckling left the poultry farm? Why or why not?

3. One theme in this story is it's better to be beautiful than to be ugly. How does this theme relate to other stories or fairy tales you have read?

Write About the Text

Writer's Checklist

- ❏ I introduced the topic and clearly stated my opinion.
- ❏ I grouped related ideas together.
- ❏ I used facts to support my opinion.
- ❏ I used linking words, including **for example**, **because**, and **in addition**, to connect my ideas.
- ❏ I have a concluding statement.

Plan your response using this graphic organizer. Use your annotations and your notes on pages 12–15 to find evidence for your essay.

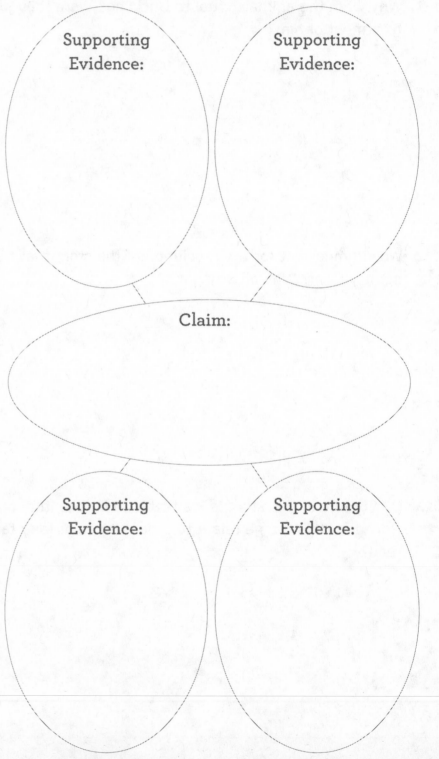

Supporting Evidence:

Supporting Evidence:

Claim:

Supporting Evidence:

Supporting Evidence:

 # Wrap Up
Check Your Understanding

1. What context clues in the text help the reader understand the meaning of the phrase <u>scoffed at</u> in paragraph 6 of the story?

    A. "beaten," "pushed," and "picked on"

    B. "ducks," "chickens," and "brothers and sisters"

    C. "the poor thing"

    D. "the whole yard"

2. This question has two parts. Answer Part A, then answer Part B.

    Part A What word best explains how the Duckling felt when he saw the swans flying overhead?

    A. jealous

    B. awed

    C. embarrassed

    D. unsure

    Part B What evidence in the text supports your answer to Part A?

    A. "The poor duckling ached with loneliness."

    B. ". . . all the miserable days and nights that Duckling had to endure . . ."

    C. ". . . uttered strange cries . . ."

    D. ". . . he loved them more than any creatures he had ever seen."

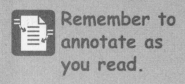
Notes

A Different Drummer by Diana Conway

1   It's raining and blowing so hard as our plane lands at the Sea-Tac Airport that all I can see out the window is a smear of colored lights. Dad hustles us along the concourse to the information board. Flight after flight is marked DELAYED, including our connection to Anchorage. Beth, Dad, and I all look at Trevor. He's been pretty good today. His only meltdown was when he had to take off his wolf hat going through security in Los Angeles. We forgot about the no-hats rule when we practiced with him at home before the trip. Trevor was fine with emptying his pockets and taking off his jacket—and since he's under twelve, he didn't have to remove his shoes—but he lives in that dumb hat and wasn't about to surrender it.

2   Mom would have wheedled Trevor into cooperating, but she wasn't with us on the return trip. Dad just said, "You are not going to hold up this long line of people," grabbed the hat, and pushed Trevor through the metal detector. Ugh! It's no fun having a ten-year-old brother who still throws tantrums like a four-year-old. It took twenty-two minutes to quiet him down. Good thing we always allow extra time when we go out in public. But our problem here is Seattle was too much time, not too little. How was Trevor going to handle the noise and confusion of stranded crowds, possibly for hours?

3   My stomach felt jittery. Besides hoping my brother wouldn't embarrass us, I was thinking about why Mom had stayed behind at Gram's house. I had overheard one of my parents' whispered conversations. "I just need a short vacation from being a mom," she said. "Can you handle the kids alone for a few days?"

Notes

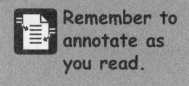
Notes

4   "No problem," Dad had said.

5   "They'll be back in school next week, and Lisa will come afternoons." Lisa is Trevor's special aide.

6   How long was a short vacation? I wondered. What if Mom decided she didn't like being a mom anymore and never came back?

7   "Dad, I'm hungry," I said. When my stomach gets all knotted up, I feed it. I guess that's why I'm the fattest one in the family.

8   We passed a frozen yogurt stand. "Ice cream!" Trevor shouted. He's as thin as a laser beam, despite his appetite.

9   "Use your inside voice," Beth said—just like Mom—but her own voice wasn't exactly quiet. The noise of crying babies and constant intercom updates made it hard for us to hear each other.

10   Dad handed me a small bag of almonds and raisins. "Let's go find someplace less crowded," he said.

11   "Ice cream," Trevor repeated.

12   "Later," Dad said. Trevor took off at a run. I started to chase him.

13   "Let him alone," Dad said. "He can't get lost here, and maybe he'll find a quiet gate to settle down at."

14   I watched Trevor dart around other kids, businesspeople in suits, parents pushing strollers, cleaning people with their wheeled trash cans, and the electronic trans that carry people who can't walk long distances. At the end of Concourse D stood floor-to-ceiling windows that overlooked the tarmac. Trevor flattened himself against the glass like a smashed bug. Freezing rain streaked down from an ominous gray sky.

Notes

15 Beth was still making her way up the slanted walkway behind us. I'm two years older than Trevor, and Beth is two years older than me. She used to be a lot of fun. Since turning fourteen, though, she prefers not to be seen with the rest of us. She found a seat as far from the windows as possible and took out her smartphone. No doubt she'd start listening to her playlist or texting all her friends.

16 Trevor was fixated on the slushy tarmac, humming as usual. Even when he was a baby, he memorized tunes instantly. I watched as he turned his wolf hat backward so he could rest his forehead on the airport window without the wolf's snout being in the way. A girl about my age walked over and stared into the yellow glass eyes. "Is that a real wolf?" she asked. Trevor ignored her. She stepped up to the window, and he quickly moved three feet to the side. "You don't have to be rude," she said.

17 I came up behind. "No, it's not real. A real wolf head would be much bigger. And he's not rude. He just needs his space."

18 The girl shook her head. "Weird!" As soon as she marched away, Trevor moved back to the exact place where he'd been standing before. My stomach cramped. I fed it the rest of the trail mix. If Mom had been here, she'd have told the girl, "Some people march to a different drummer."

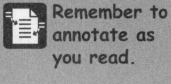
Notes

19   But Mom wasn't here, and Dad was standing by the airline agent at gate D-20, keeping an eye on us from a distance. I sat down in the row of seats nearest Trevor's window and took out the anime book Mom had given me for the trip home. Soon I was deep in outer space and far away from family worries.

20   Sometime later I became aware of a low-grade roar around me. Almost all the surrounding seats had filled up. Babies wailed, toddlers fussed, older kids whined, parents scolded, and teenagers' earbuds leaked loud music. Quickly I looked for Trevor. He wasn't at the window. I couldn't see his wolf hat sticking up over any seats. Beth still sat in her far-off corner, but where was Dad?

21   I put my book away and stood up. I had turned almost a complete circle when I finally spotted Trevor. He was sitting on the gray carpet in the exact center of the waiting area, holding his new wooden flute. Three days ago we had all gone with Gram to a Renaissance fair. Beth and I were impatient to mingle with pretend knights and ladies, eat meat-filled pastries, and watch mock sword fights, magic acts, and old-fashioned dances. Trevor immediately fixated on a musical instrument booth, where a man sat on a high stool wearing a jester's cap and playing a soprano recorder. Behind him hung dulcimers, zithers, flutes, cymbals, and other handmade instruments. Trevor refused to move.

22   You could have heard Mom's sigh across the whole grassy field of striped tents. "I'll stay with Trevor," she said. "You all go ahead and enjoy the fair." Three hours later we found them still there. I suppose that's when Mom decided she needed her own vacation.

Notes

23 Now, here in the airport, Trevor put his new recorder to his lips and blew a shrill sound. My stomach fell. All these tired people around, and he had to start a disturbance!

24 Trevor shook his head. He took a couple of slow breaths. The next time he puckered his lips around the mouthpiece, a gentle breathy sound came out. Then another a little higher up the scale. Finally a whole series of birdlike trills. Two pig-tailed sisters wearing identical polka-dotted dresses sat down on the floor facing Trevor. Some slightly taller boys stood watching. A father rolled his baby over in a stroller. Before you could say "Pied Piper," a crowd had gathered to listen. I picked out Dad by his red plaid vest and joined him.

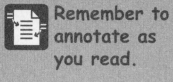
Notes

25   How did Trevor know which fingers to lift at the right time to make a different tone—sometimes one, other times two or three? I've taken piano lessons for two years and still can't play anything without reading music. Trevor just seems to know which fingers to put where—on the piano at home as well as here on his recorder. He seems to have all the music in his head. I recognized snatches of childhood songs like "Twinkle, Twinkle, Little Star," "Three Blind Mice," and "Frère Jacques," but mostly he was making up tunes that rippled gently through the stagnant air.

26   After a half hour or so he stopped to rest. A woman with silvery hair clapped softly. "That was beautiful," she said. More people applauded, and a couple of them cried out, "Encore!" Someone asked how long he'd been taking lessons. Trevor started a new tune without answering the question. Nobody moved away.

27   Even the sun seemed to want to listen to the music. The big windows that looked out on the tarmac suddenly became much brighter. No longer was snow and rain beating against the glass. A chirpy voice came over the intercom to announce that the airport had been reopened and flights would begin to board very soon.

28   Beth came over to show us the minivideo of Trevor's music that she'd just e-mailed Mom on her phone. Dad said we still had an hour before our flight, and who wanted ice cream? Trevor shoved his recorder in his backpack and took off at a run for the frozen yogurt stand.

29   Mom's answering text came in on Beth's phone while our family hunched at a little table licking cones. DIFFERENT DRUMMER GRAM N I HAVIN FUN MIS U ALL. HOME FRI

30   "Gooood," Trevor said.

31   Maybe, like me, he was thinking about all of us being together again, but with my brother, you never know. It could just be his way of saying that chocolate raspberry swirl is the very best flavor in the world.

Notes

Close Reading and Collaborative Conversations

What Does the Text Say?	How Does the Text Work?
1. In three sentences or less, summarize "A Different Drummer." Then share your summary with a partner.	**1.** What details in the text help the reader picture the scene at the airport?
2. What important information does the reader learn about Trevor in the first two paragraphs?	**2.** Reread paragraphs 16–18. Why are these paragraphs important to the story?
3. What family members are traveling together? Why is the mother not there?	**3.** In paragraph 23, the narrator says, "My stomach fell." What emotion does that convey? Use details from the text to support your answer.

What Does the Text Mean?

1. What do Trevor and Duckling from "The Not-So-Ugly Duckling" have in common? How does each story reveal the trait they share?

2. Trevor marches to "a different drummer." What does this metaphor mean within the context of the story? How can this metaphor be applied to "Narcissa," the poem at the beginning of this unit?

3. The narrator describes several problems in this story. Are all the problems resolved at the end of the story? Use details from the text to support your opinion.

Write About the Text

Informative/ Explanatory Writing Prompt

After reading "A Different Drummer," write an essay answering the question: How does Trevor show that he marches to "a different drummer" more than most other people? Support your answer with evidence from the text.

Writer's Checklist

❏ I introduced the topic.

❏ I used facts and examples to develop the topic.

❏ I used linking words, such as **another**, **for example**, and **also**, to connect ideas.

❏ I used precise language.

❏ I have a concluding statement.

Plan your essay using this graphic organizer. Use your annotations and your notes on pages 18–27 to find evidence for your essay.

Introduction:

Text Evidence:

Text Evidence:

Text Evidence:

Conclusion:

 # Wrap Up
Check Your Understanding

1. What phrase describes the meaning of the word <u>surrender</u> as it is used in paragraph 1?

   A. give up being difficult to his family

   B. give up the hat to airport security for scanning

   C. give up thinking that his hat is dumb

   D. give up the hat to an opposing army

2. This question has two parts. Answer Part A, then answer Part B.

   Part A What is Beth's main role in the family during this story? How does she relate to her siblings?

   A. She wants to keep the family together all the time.

   B. She wants to separate herself from her family.

   C. She makes sure that everyone in the family is having fun.

   D. She wishes that she were with her mom rather than her dad and siblings.

   Part B What evidence in the text supports your answer to Part A?

   A. "Beth and I were impatient to mingle with pretend knights and ladies."

   B. "Since turning fourteen, though, she prefers not to be seen with the rest of us."

   C. "Beth came over to show us the minivideo of Trevor's music that she'd just e-mailed Mom on her phone."

   D. "'Use your inside voice,' Beth said—just like Mom—but her own voice wasn't exactly quiet."

 Wrap Up

Check Your Understanding

3. What theme is the narrator sharing in the last paragraph?

"Maybe, like me, he was thinking about all of us being together again, but with my brother, you never know. It could just be his way of saying that chocolate raspberry swirl is the very best flavor in the world."

A. When someone marches to their own drummer, you never really know what they are thinking.

B. Sometimes, food is more important than anything else, even family.

C. It's not important whether or not people in a family care about each other.

D. Raspberry swirl is a flavor that can make kids stop making sense.

4. What do the characters Narcissa, from the poem, and Trevor have in common?

A. Both are loners who don't interact much with other people in terms of playing or conversation.

B. Both need to be taken care of by their families because they are not always socially appropriate.

C. Both are extremely imaginative, and live in a fantasy world.

D. Both are very musical, and can impress others with their talents.

Accessing Complex Texts Now! • Grade 5 • ©2014 Benchmark Education Company, LLC

Read and Write Across Texts

Plan your essay using this graphic organizer. Use your annotations and the notes you've taken on each passage to identify supporting evidence for your essay.

Introduction:

Evidence from "Narcissa":

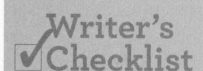

Informative/ Explanatory Writing Prompt

Each text focuses on characters that are different, yet they find places to be happy. Examine Narcissa, Duckling, and Trevor to analyze the different ways they find their own place in the world. Use examples from the texts in your essay.

Writer's Checklist

❏ I introduced the topic.

❏ I used facts and examples to develop the topic.

❏ I used linking words, such as **another**, **for example**, and **also**, to connect ideas.

❏ I used precise language.

❏ I have a concluding statement.

Evidence from "The Not-So-Ugly Duckling":

Evidence from "A Different Drummer":

Conclusion:

Unit 2

Ecosystems

Table of Contents

Notes

•Foul Ball•

1   When people think of plants, they think green. The green of plants comes from special green cell parts called chloroplasts. Most plants use chloroplasts to make food from sunlight. But not the stinking corpse lily. The corpse lily doesn't have any chloroplasts, and it doesn't need sunlight. It steals its food instead.

2   Most of the time, the stinking corpse lily hides down in the earth, clinging to the roots and stem of a host plant. The lily sucks out sugars that the host plant makes for itself. The rainforests where the stinking corpse lily lives are filled with tall, leafy trees. All those trees make a lot of shade, so very little sunlight reaches the forest floor. Stealing food lets the stinking corpse lily survive where it's too dark for other plants.

3   The corpse lily can only be seen when it flowers. The flower buds erupt from the plant's root. They swell to the size of basketballs and then open their petals. The flowers can be over three feet (one meter) wide. That's so big that a toddler could stretch out on them like a bed. But you wouldn't want to nap there! As the name suggests, stinking corpse lilies are famous for smelling like dead, rotting animals.

Notes

4   The lily uses its horrible smell to attract flies. When flies smell the corpse lily, they come to check it out. As they walk around the flower looking for the rotting meat, they get covered in pollen. The disappointed flies carry the pollen away with them when they leave. If the plant is lucky, the flies will be fooled by another corpse flower soon and drop the pollen off there.

5   The corpse lily is an exception to the rule that all plants photosynthesize. Why bother, when you can make such a lovely smell without all that work?

It may look pretty, but the corpse lily doesn't smell pretty.

Close Reading and Collaborative Conversations

What Does the Text Say?	How Does the Text Work?
1. What general information does the author want you to know? Turn to a partner and summarize "Foul Ball."	**1.** In paragraph 3, find the word "erupt." What does it usually mean? What does it mean in the context of this text? Explain your reasoning.
2. How does the corpse lily get food?	**2.** What is the author's tone in this passage? How does the author establish the tone?
3. What makes the corpse lily different from other plants?	**3.** How does the author organize this passage? Use details from the text to support your answer.

What Does the Text Mean?

1. Explain how the author supports the idea that the corpse lily is "an exception to the rule that all plants photosynthesize."

2. Why did the author entitle this text "Foul Ball"? Explain the reasoning using evidence from the text.

3. Based on what you know about plants, do you think that the corpse lily is actually "stealing" and that its scent is "horrible"? Why do you think the author uses those words to describe the corpse lily?

Write About the Text

Informative/ Explanatory Writing Prompt

After reading "Foul Ball," write an essay explaining the main difference between the corpse lily and other plants. Use examples from the text to explain your answer.

Writer's Checklist

- ❏ I introduced the topic.

- ❏ I used facts and examples to develop the topic.

- ❏ I used linking works, such as **another**, **for example**, and **also**, to connect ideas.

- ❏ I used precise language.

- ❏ I have a concluding statement.

Plan your response using this graphic organizer. Use your annotations and your notes on pages 34–37 to identify supporting evidence.

Introduction:

Example:

Supporting Text Evidence:

Example:

Supporting Text Evidence:

Conclusion:

# Wrap Up
Check Your Understanding

1. This question has two parts. Answer Part A, then answer Part B.

Part A How large is the flower of the corpse lily once it expands?

  A. as large as a basketball

  B. as large as a toddler

  C. as large as an adult-size bed

  D. as large as a corpse

Part B What does the author accomplish by using this comparison?

  A. The author is scaring the readers so that they imagine a dead person in a flower.

  B. The author is explaining that if not for the stink, the corpse lily would be a comfortable bed.

  C. The author is explaining that the corpse lily flowers in an unusual ball-shape.

  D. The author is allowing the reader to consider a known size when imagining the lily.

2. What purpose does the author have for explaining that the corpse lily doesn't have chloroplasts?

  A. The purpose is to explain why the flower has such a disgusting smell.

  B. The purpose is to explain why it doesn't need the sun and must have another food source.

  C. The purpose is to explain why the corpse lily lives on the forest floor instead of in its canopy.

  D. The purpose is to explain that the corpse lily has a lot in common with other plants.

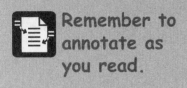
Notes

Oysters:
Ecosystem Engineers

1   Scientists have called oysters "ecosystem engineers." What is it that makes this simple shellfish so important?

2   Oysters are found in shallow saltwater bays and lagoons. They can also live in estuaries and marshes, which are places where saltwater meets freshwater. Oysters can survive a range of climates from the chilly New England coast to the warmer Gulf of Mexico.

3   Oysters live in large colonies called beds or reefs. Since the oysters can't build on mud, they start a reef by attaching to rocks or a hard surface. As the oysters multiply, they grow on the shells of other oysters. Hundreds of years ago, oyster reefs would grow so large that ships had to navigate around them.

4   Oyster reefs provide a habitat for many species of invertebrates, such as shrimp, clams, snails, and crabs, as well as many species of fish. They are a source of food for birds and other marine life. Beth Ravit, an environmental scientist and professor at Rutgers University, says that oysters are "a cold water version of a coral reef. They create a home and a restaurant for other species to live and eat."

Notes

5   In addition to providing food and a place to live, oysters play another important role in their ecosystem. Oysters are filter feeders. They live on algae, zooplankton, phytoplankton, and bacteria that float in the ocean water. Oysters open their shells and use tiny cilia to draw in plankton, sediment, and other particles over their gills. Then they spit out cleaner water. A single oyster can clean up to 50 gallons of water a day. Beth Ravit says, "These ecological engineers work round the clock filtering water. They literally change, physically and chemically, the system they are a part of."

6   Oysters help to remove the cloudiness from the water. This allows sea grass and other plant species to thrive. According to scientist Ravit, this process puts oxygen into the water, promotes photosynthesis, and creates conditions by which other marine species can live. Oysters help retain the balance of the ecosystem.

7   Unfortunately, there has been a dramatic decline in the oyster population. Globally, 85% of oyster reefs have been lost. This makes oyster reefs the most severely impacted marine habitat on Earth.

8   Overfishing, pollution, habitat loss, and disease are all causes for the decline. People have been harvesting oysters for hundreds of years. But as fishing methods grew more sophisticated, more oysters were taken each year than could be replaced. In addition, habitat was lost as estuaries were filled in. Pollution made it impossible for oysters to survive in some waters.

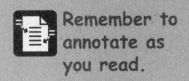

Notes

The oyster is called a bivalve because it has two shells that are connected with a small hinge. It opens its shell to take in food and expel waste. It can close its shell if threatened.

9   But today, both the government and environmental groups are working to bring back the oyster population. Projects are underway in Maryland, North Carolina, Florida, Texas, New York, and many other places to restore oyster reefs.

10   The National Oceanic and Atmospheric Administration is working to bring oysters back to Chesapeake Bay. Scientists are raising oyster larvae in laboratories. Then they place the larvae in large tanks that are filled with oyster shells. The larvae attach themselves to the shells. Then the shells are dumped into reef areas in the bay. The goal is to create 97 acres of oyster reefs in one part of Chesapeake Bay.

11   In Florida, the Nature Conservancy is using oyster mats to increase the oyster population. Oyster shells are tied to mesh mats. Then the mats are placed in the Indian River Lagoon, an estuary. The idea is that oysters can build new reefs on the mats. Volunteers tie the oyster shells to the mats. So far, about 20,000 mats have been placed in the water and 22 acres of reef have been created in the estuary.

12   In New York, people are even trying to bring back oysters to parts of New York Harbor. They hope the oysters can help clean the polluted harbors. One plan is to create a living reef at the mouth of the city's Gowanus Canal. This area was once filled with oysters. But now they have mostly disappeared. This body of water is one of the most polluted in the United States. In addition, the canal was dredged to create shipping lanes. The digging destroyed the hard, rocky surfaces oysters attach themselves to.

13   To reintroduce the oysters to the canal, a raft with an oyster nursery below will be created. This will help the oyster eggs to mature. Then, woven nets will be placed in the harbor to give the oysters something to attach to.

14   All of these programs have succeeded in increasing the oyster population. But there is still a lot of work to be done.

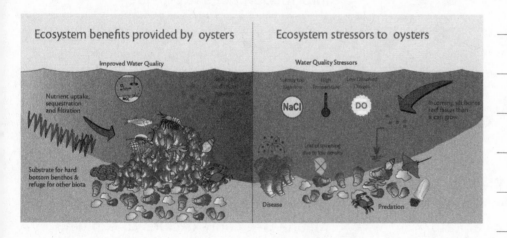

Close Reading and Collaborative Conversations

What Does the Text Say?	How Does the Text Work?
1. What is this text mostly about? Turn to a partner and summarize "Oysters: Ecosystem Engineers."	**1.** What is the author's purpose in paragraphs 4–6?
2. What problems do oyster reefs face?	**2.** How does the diagram on page 43 help support the text in this passage? What additional information does it provide?
3. What artificial measures are scientists taking to reintroduce the oysters to their former habitats?	**3.** Look at the word "navigate" in paragraph 3. What does this word mean? Use context clues to explain.

What Does the Text Mean?

1. This text aims to inform the reader about oysters, but it also has a persuasive element. What is the author trying to convince the reader of?

2. The corpse lily and the oyster are very different. Both are impressive. What makes each an impressive organism?

3. Both "Oysters: Ecosystem Engineers" and "Foul Ball" focus on a single organism—oysters and corpse lilies. How are the texts structured similarly or differently?

Write About the Text

Opinion/Argument Writing Prompt

After reading "Oysters: Ecosystem Engineers," write an essay answering this question: Is saving oyster reefs essential to the environment? Support your opinion with evidence from the text.

Writer's Checklist

- ❏ I introduced the topic and clearly stated my opinion.

- ❏ I grouped related ideas together.

- ❏ I used facts to support my opinion.

- ❏ I used linking words, such as **for example**, **because**, and **in addition**, to connect my ideas.

- ❏ I have a concluding statement.

Plan your response using this graphic organizer. Use your annotations and your notes on pages 40–45 to identify supporting evidence.

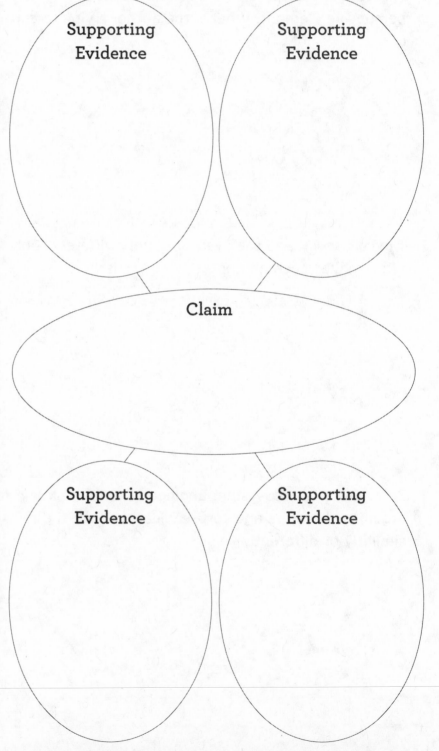

Supporting Evidence

Supporting Evidence

Claim

Supporting Evidence

Supporting Evidence

# Wrap Up
Check Your Understanding

1. What context clues in the text help the reader understand the meaning of the phrase <u>filter feeders</u> in the second sentence of paragraph 5?

    A. "spit out cleaner water"

    B. "live on algae, zooplankton, phytoplankton, and bacteria"

    C. "providing food and a place to live"

    D. "play another important role in their ecosystem"

2. This question has two parts. Answer Part A, then answer Part B.

Part A What is a main idea of the text?

    A. Oysters are one of the most unusual creatures in the sea.

    B. Oysters play a helpful and important role in their ecosystem.

    C. Oysters have contributed to overfishing and pollution.

    D. Oysters need more people to volunteer to save them.

Part B What evidence in the text supports the answer you chose?

    A. "Overfishing, pollution, habitat loss, and disease are all causes for the decline."

    B. "Volunteers tie the oyster shells to the mats."

    C. "The oyster is called a bivalve because it has two shells that are connected with a small hinge."

    D. "Oysters are 'a cold water version of a coral reef.'"

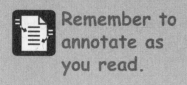
Notes

Oceans
_of_
Grass

by Kathleen Weidner Zoehfeld

1   Seeing the vast North American Prairie for the first time in 1805, the explorer Meriwether Lewis described it in his diary as "beautiful in the extreme." Imagine going back 200 years, to the time of Lewis and Clark. You saddle up your horse, hop aboard a flatboat, and cross the Mississippi River toward the little trading post known as St. Louis.

2   You step out on the western bank and begin to ride. All around you stretches an endless ocean of grass, rippling in the wind. At first the grass is so tall, you're barely high enough to see above it, even on horseback.

3   Continue to ride west and you will notice the grass becoming shorter. Now it only brushes against your ankles or knee. Colorful wildflowers bloom in abundance, but there are hardly any trees or bushes. The few trees you do see grow only along rivers or streams. Farther west the land gets drier, with short grasses clinging to the rolling hills like a carpet. After many weeks on horseback, you finally see the Rocky Mountains looming on the western horizon.

4   For the explorers of the early 1800s who had spent their entire lives in the rolling woodlands of the east, these endless grass-covered plains were astonishing. West of the Mississippi, America seemed to be a land entirely of grass.

Got Water?

5   Grasslands cover more than one-quarter of the earth's land. They are found on every continent except Antarctica and go by many names. Prairie, veld, savanna, steppe—all mean a lot of grass.

6   Though they may look lush and green, grasslands are actually quite dry. In fact, grasslands spring up where there is too little water for trees. Trees need a lot of rain, but grass is well adapted to dry conditions.

7   Different kinds of grasses grow in different climates. Tallgrass prairies and savannas, a mix of grass and trees, grow where there is a modest amount of water, though not enough for a forest. In drier areas, mixed-grass, or medium height, prairies take over. Shortgrass prairies are the driest of all.

8   Weather on the broad open plains can be extreme. Summers are often blazing hot, while in winter freezing winds howl across the landscape. Long periods of drought are common. Winds blow constantly.

Grasslands receive an average of 10 to 35 inches of rain a year.

Notes

Remember to annotate as you read.

Notes

9   This harsh weather can be very hard on trees. But wild grasses are as tough as nails. They bend and sway easily in the wind, and are well adapted to survive droughts, fierce storms, and extreme heat and cold.

10   For one thing, grasses are water conservation experts. All plants have tiny openings in their leaves, called stomata, through which they take in carbon dioxide from the air. But plants also lose water through these openings. Broad leaves, like those on trees, would dry out in the fierce sun and wind of the prairie. But grasses have narrow leaves, called blades, with few stomata. Grasses also close their stomata in the mid-day sun, opening them up again in the cool evening.

11   Prairie grasses have very deep roots, which can reach far down to find hidden water. In fact, the part you see above ground is only about a third of the grass plant. Grasses grow from the bottom upward, not out from the top like a tree. In winter or after a fire, the leaves and stems shrivel up, but the grasses' growing roots remain vital and alive. As soon as the rains return, the grasses spring into action, sending out fresh shoots, stems, and leaves. All this makes prairie grasses very hard to kill.

12   Even fires can't keep grasses down for long. Lightning frequently starts prairie fires in old, dried-up grass. But with their roots safe underground, grasses soon recover.

13   In fact, fire even helps the grasses by clearing the area of any young trees or bushes that might block their light or steal their water.

How to Make a Prairie

14   Fifty million years ago, after the time of the dinosaurs, the earth's climate was hot and humid. The land that is now the North American Prairie was a tropical rainforest. But for millions of years, Earth's crust had been crumpling up to make the Rocky Mountains. The Rockies grew so high they began to block air blowing in from the Pacific Ocean, and the land to the east of the mountains grew drier.

15   Then, about two million years ago, a permanent winter settled in over the plains. Huge ice sheets called glaciers, up to two miles thick, covered the land. The glaciers advanced and retreated many times, bringing rocks, gravel, and silt from the north, smoothing out the land and building up a rich layer of black soil. When the glaciers finally melted, wet spruce forests with patchy meadows sprang up. Mammoths, giant sloths, saber-toothed cats, and American cheetahs moved in, as did the ancestors of bison and pronghorn antelope. Gradually, as the last Ice Age ended, the land dried up. By 10,000 years ago, most of the Ice Age animals were extinct. The spruce forests disappeared, and grasses gradually took over—giving us the prairie we see today.

Notes

With their roots safe underground, scorched grasses soon recover.

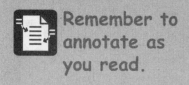

Notes

Home on the Range

16 Like all green plants, grasses use the energy of the sun to make sugar out of water, carbon dioxide from the air, and minerals from the soil. Grasses store that sugar in their roots, stems, leaves and seeds.

17 Every animal on the prairie depends on the grass for food. And all that grass supports a rich variety of life. The biggest animals on the prairie are the wandering grazers, such as elk, bison, and cattle. They nibble the grasses right down to their roots. But that doesn't hurt the grasses. When the herds move on, the grass grows right back. Many insects eat grass, too, or sip the nectar of prairie wildflowers. Birds, mice, gophers, badgers, and toads feast on abundant bugs, and themselves provide food for hunting snakes, coyotes, wolves, and owls.

18 In these treeless landscapes, many animals are burrowers. Prairie dogs and pocket gophers dig huge tunnel cities and feed on roots that grow down through the roof.

19 Small owls, rabbits, turtles, and snakes often move into these burrows, too. Some animals make their homes in the grass itself, nestling into the dry tufts to hide from prowling hawks.

20 Under the prairie, earthworms, beetles, bacteria, and fungi are hard at work breaking down dead plants and animals. These decomposers recycle nutrients so they can be used again, building up new layers for topsoil from which grasses and flowers can grow.

21 Every grassland has its own special mix of animals, big and small, but grasses feed them all.

Plowing the Prairie

22   Grasses feed us, too! When Lewis and Clark went west in 1805, they met bears, wolves, badgers, and herds of bison so large they took days to pass by. The explorers also met tribes of native people who followed the bison across the plains. If Lewis and Clark came back today, they might not recognize the place. Nearly every square foot of the tallgrass prairie has been plowed and turned into cropland. Cows and sheep graze on the shortgrass prairie, once the home of the bison and pronghorn. The wild wolves, bears, and bison have retreated to national parks.

23   But though it looks very different, the prairie is still all grass. The grains that now fill the prairie are all grasses that people have specially bred to bear extra-big seeds. The roots of these grain grasses don't grow as deep as those of wild grasses, so they are not as tough and need more water. But grains grow well in the rich prairie soil and provide food for millions of people around the world. The North American Prairie has changed a lot over its long history, but the ocean of grass waves on.

Notes

Farm animals now graze on the shortgrass prairies.

Close Reading and Collaborative Conversations

What Does the Text Say?	How Does the Text Work?
1. What is the big idea in this text? Turn to a partner and summarize "Oceans of Grass."	**1.** Reread paragraphs 1 to 4. What is the author's purpose in these paragraphs? How do they relate to the main idea?
2. Explain why some areas have long grasses and others have short grasses.	**2.** In paragraph 17, the author uses the word "abundant." Explain what this word means using context clues.
3. Why did there used to be forests in the area that is now the plains?	**3.** How does the author organize the information in this text?

What Does the Text Mean?

1. In paragraph 9, the author calls wild grasses "tough as nails." What reasons and evidence does she give to support that point?

2. What are a few of the main differences between how this author explores the role of organisms in an ecosystem and how the authors of the other two passages in this unit approach the topic?

3. Would the author of this text say that the changing of the grasslands to farmlands is a good or bad thing? Use evidence from the text to explain.

Write About the Text

Informative/ Explanatory Writing Prompt

After reading "Oceans of Grass," write an essay answering this question: How do wild grasses respond to changes in their environment, such as the availability of water? Support your discussion with evidence from the text.

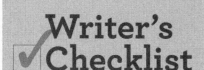

Writer's Checklist

❏ I introduced the topic.

❏ I used facts and examples to develop the topic.

❏ I used linking works, such as **another**, **for example**, and **also**, to connect ideas.

❏ I used precise language.

❏ I have a concluding statement.

Plan your response using this graphic organizer. Use your annotations and your notes on pages 48–55 to identify supporting evidence for your essay.

Topic:

Details:

Explain:

Detail:

Explain:

Conclusion:

# Wrap Up
Check Your Understanding

1. Pick two statements that accurately describe the grassland ecosystem.

   A. Grasslands go by the names of prairie, veld, savanna, and steppe and cover more than one-quarter of Earth's land.

   B. Grasslands are fragile ecosystems that struggle when faced with droughts.

   C. Grasslands can recover from wildfires.

   D. Grasslands were caused by the development of an ice age.

2. This question has two parts. Answer Part A, then answer Part B.

   Part A In paragraph 19, what does the word <u>burrows</u> mean?

   A. grassy nests on the ground

   B. holes dug into the ground

   C. buildings above the ground

   D. nests made out of roots

   Part B What evidence from the text best supports your answer?

   A. "dig huge tunnel"

   B. "cities"

   C. "home in the grass itself"

   D. "feed on roots"

# Wrap Up
Check Your Understanding

3. This question has two parts. Answer Part A, then answer Part B.

Part A Which statement below would the author agree with?

 A. Grasslands are more important than forest environments.

 B. Grasslands support a wide range of species.

 C. The plains are home to many unusual animals.

 D. The plains look much the same as they did 200 years ago.

Part B What evidence from the text best supports your answer?

 A. ". . . all that grass supports a rich variety of life."

 B. "Mammoths, giant sloths, saber-toothed cats, and American cheetahs moved in . . ."

 C. "The North American Prairie has changed a lot over its long history, but the ocean of grass waves on."

 D. "In fact, fire even helps the grasses by clearing the area of any young trees or bushes that might block their light or steal their water."

Read and Write Across Texts

Plan your response using this graphic organizer.
Use your annotations and the notes you've taken on each
passage to identify supporting evidence for your essay.

Introduction:

Evidence from "Foul Ball":

Informative/ Explanatory Writing Prompt

Each of these informational texts gives information about how a type of organism fits into its ecosystem. Explain how each of these organisms relates to its environment differently. Support your writing with text evidence.

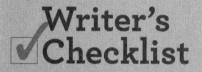 # Writer's Checklist

☐ I introduced the topic.

☐ I used facts and examples to develop the topic.

☐ I used linking works, such as **another, for example**, and **also**, to connect ideas.

☐ I used precise language.

☐ I have a concluding statement.

Evidence from "Oysters: Ecosystem Engineers":

Evidence from "Oceans of Grass":

Conclusion:

Unit 3
Independence

③ Independence

Table of Contents

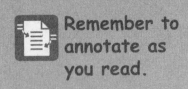
Notes

The French and Indian War
~ Sets the Stage ~
for the Revolution

1   In 1754, a war broke out between Britain and France. They were fighting over land in North America. Britain wanted to gain control of an area west of the Alleghany Mountains. The war ended in 1763. Britain won control of the land. The aftermath of the war affected both the British government and the American colonists. In many ways, it put them on a path to the American Revolution.

2   Fighting the French and Indian War was very expensive. The British government had borrowed money and needed to pay it back. In addition, the British had gained a lot of land from the French in North America, including many forts. They stationed British soldiers in the forts, which cost a lot of money. The British government decided to start taxing the American colonists, which they had not done before. The first taxes were the Sugar Act of 1763 and the Stamp Act of 1764.

3   The American colonists didn't think the taxes were fair because they had no elected representatives in the British government. The colonists protested the taxes and the British government did away with them. However, the British government thought it had the power to tax the colonists, so they voted for another tax. After the American colonists protested, they did away with that one, too. This went on for about ten years.

Adapted from The National Park Service's Teacher Education Kit

Notes

4   In 1773, the British government passed a tax on tea. In protest, colonists in Massachusetts dumped chests of tea into the harbor. The British government became angry. They decided to punish the colony by closing the port of Boston. They also took away much of Massachusetts's power to govern itself. Many American colonists didn't think the British government had the right to do these things. In the fall of 1774, twelve of the colonies decided to send representatives to a meeting of the first Continental Congress. They wanted to coordinate their opposition to the British government.

5   In the past, the colonies had acted independently, but things were changing. During the French and Indian War, the American colonists had fought together under the command of the British military. At the Continental Congress, the colonists came together to protest how the British government was treating them.

6   In April 1775, the first shots of the American Revolution were fired. The second Continental Congress met and appointed George Washington as the commander of the American army.

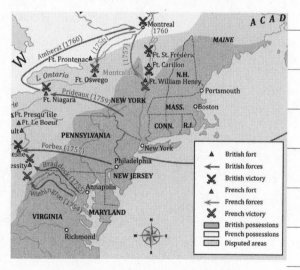

The Americans tried to resolve their disagreement with the British government, but they could not find a solution. On July 4, 1776, the colonists issued the Declaration of Independence, stating that they planned to break away from the British and form their own government.

Close Reading and Collaborative Conversations

What Does the Text Say?	How Does the Text Work?
1. What is the text mostly about? Turn to a partner and summarize "The French and Indian War Sets the Stage for the Revolution."	**1.** How does the author support the point that the American colonists didn't think the British taxes were fair?
2. How did the tax on tea in 1773 affect the relationship between the American colonists and the British government?	**2.** How does the author help readers understand the timing of events beginning with the French and Indian War and ending with the American Revolution?
3. How did the French and Indian War relate to the American Revolution?	**3.** Reread paragraphs 5 and 6 and define the word "revolution." What context clues help you figure out its meaning?

What Does the Text Mean?

1. What inference can you make about how the British government felt about the American colonies? Use text evidence to support your answer.

2. After reading the text, why do you think it was important for the American colonists to protest the British taxes?

3. Why was it important that the colonists fought together during the French and Indian War? Use details from the text to support your answer.

Write About the Text

Writer's ☑ Checklist

- ❏ I introduced the topic.
- ❏ I used facts and examples to develop the topic.
- ❏ I used linking works, such as **another**, **for example**, and **also**, to connect ideas.
- ❏ I used precise language.
- ❏ I have a concluding statement.

Plan your response using this graphic organizer. Use your annotations and your notes on pages 62–65 to find text evidence for your essay.

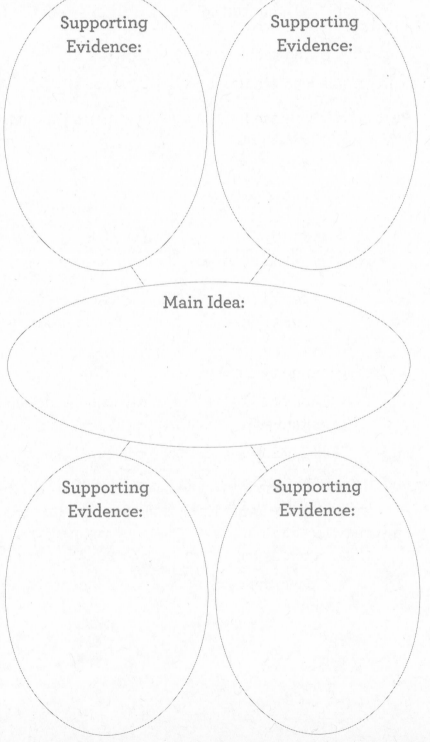

Supporting Evidence:

Supporting Evidence:

Main Idea:

Supporting Evidence:

Supporting Evidence:

Wrap Up
Check Your Understanding

1. This question has two parts. Answer Part A, then answer Part B.

   Part A What is the meaning of the word <u>representatives</u> in paragraph 4?

   A. people who protest taxes

   B. people who are colonists

   C. people who speak for others

   D. people who are upset about unfair laws

   Part B Which phrase from paragraph 4 helps you understand the meaning of <u>representatives</u>?

   A. "passed a tax"

   B. "twelve of the colonies decided to send"

   C. "took away much of Massachusetts's power"

   D. "the British government had the right"

2. Choose three sentences the author uses to show how the colonies were working together to oppose the unfair British government.

   ☐ "The American colonists didn't think the taxes were fair because they had no elected representatives in the British government."

   ☐ "In the fall of 1774, twelve of the colonies decided to send representatives to a meeting of the first Continental Congress."

   ☐ "In April 1775, the first shots of the American Revolution were fired."

   ☐ "However, the British government thought it had the power to tax the colonists, so they voted for another tax."

   ☐ "The second Continental Congress met and appointed George Washington as the commander of the American army."

   ☐ "In the past, the colonies had acted independently, but things were changing."

Notes

A Magical Pen
by Ruth Spencer Johnson

Cast:

Thomas Jefferson
His grandchildren:
    Ellen, age 14
    Virginia, age 9
    Mary, age 7
    James, age 4
Narrator

(One evening at Monticello, Thomas Jefferson sits in the parlor as some of his grandchildren dance around him. Red curtains drape over the tops of tall windows. The floor is parquet—pieces of wood that fit together to make a pattern.)

1 **Narrator:** After two terms as president of the United States, Thomas Jefferson has retired to Monticello. Here in the parlor, Thomas loves to play games and music with his daughter Martha's children. *(Jefferson's young granddaughter Mary climbs onto his lap.)*

2 **Mary:** Grandpapa, please tell us the story of how you wrote the Declaration of Independence!

3 **Narrator:** Remember, during the American Revolution, the Continental Congress met in Philadelphia and decided that the thirteen American Colonies should separate from England. The Declaration of Independence is the famous document stating why America should be a free and independent country.

Accessing Complex Texts Now! • Grade 5 • ©2014 Benchmark Education Company, LLC

Notes

4 **Jefferson:** Why, you children have heard me tell that story many times!

5 **Ellen:** I never get tired of hearing it, Grandpapa.

6 **Jefferson:** Well, all right. *(Ellen, Virginia, and James sit on the floor in front of Jefferson.)* On June 11, 1776, the Continental Congress put me on a committee of five people to write the Declaration. The committee met, and we talked over ideas for the document.

7 **Virginia:** Ben Franklin and John Adams were on the committee, too.

8 **Narrator:** Notice the paintings of famous people, such as Franklin and Adams, covering the parlor walls?

9 **Jefferson:** The committee asked me to write a rough draft of the Declaration. I was one of the youngest members of Congress, only thirty-three, but I said I would do my best.

10 **James:** Why did the committee choose you?

11 **Jefferson:** They said I was the best writer—that I had a "masterly pen."

12 **Mary:** John Adams said you could write ten times better than he could!

Remember to annotate as you read.

Notes

13 **Narrator:** Over the next seventeen days, Jefferson worked on the Declaration whenever he wasn't busy in Congress. He wrote the document on a portable writing desk he had designed himself.

14 **Ellen:** How did you decide what to write?

15 **Jefferson:** I believed with all my heart that America should be a free nation. I tried to make that idea so plain and clear that anyone reading the Declaration would have to agree.

16 **Virginia:** You wrote that all men are born free and equal. And people have the right to control their own lives.

17 **Ellen:** You listed the Colonies' complaints against England and explained why Americans wanted independence.

18 **Jefferson:** I hoped to inspire my countrymen with my words, but I had to work quickly. Congress was in a hurry to get the document.

19 **James:** What happened next?

20 **Jefferson:** I showed my rough draft to the committee, and they made a few changes. Overall, I think they were pleased with my work.

21 **Narrator:** Jefferson presented the Declaration to Congress. On July 2, Congress voted for independence from England. Then the delegates began to go over the Declaration, line by line.

22 **Mary:** The delegates thought your writing was beautiful, didn't they?

23 **Jefferson:** Well, they certainly argued about it—for almost three days! They changed words and cut out some parts, but most of the wording was still my own.

24 **Virginia:** Did the changes hurt your feelings, Grandpapa?

25 **Jefferson:** It was painful to listen as the delegates criticized the document I had worked so hard on.

26 **Narrator:** On July 4, Congress approved the final version of the Declaration. That's why we celebrate America's birthday on the fourth of July.

27 **Ellen:** You should be proud—the Declaration of Independence inspired people to fight for freedom.

28 **Virginia:** With your pen, you took ordinary words and turned them into something special—almost like magic!

29 **James:** Grandpapa, you must have a magical pen! (*Everyone laughs.*)

30 **Jefferson:** Now, children, let's light the candles and find a book to read. You know I just can't live without books!

Notes

Independence

Close Reading and Collaborative Conversations

What Does the Text Say?	How Does the Text Work?
1. What is the play mostly about? Turn to a partner and summarize "A Magical Pen."	**1.** What is the narrator's job in the play?
2. How did Thomas Jefferson respond to the challenge of writing such an important document?	**2.** How do the stage directions help you understand what is happening in the play?
3. Why did the delegates argue over Jefferson's writing?	**3.** How do Thomas Jefferson's grandchildren's points of view influence the scene?

What Does the Text Mean?

1. After reading Passages 1 and 2, what inference can you make about how the American colonists felt about Thomas Jefferson? Use text evidence to support your answer.

2. What kind of a person was Thomas Jefferson? Use details from the play to support your opinion.

3. James says, "Grandpapa, you must have a magical pen!" What does he mean by that? Do you agree or disagree with his description? Support your answers with details from the text.

Write About the Text

After reading "A Magical Pen," write two paragraphs explaining the process Thomas Jefferson went through as he wrote the Declaration of Independence. Support your discussion with evidence from the play.

Writer's ☑Checklist

❏ I introduced the topic.

❏ I used facts and examples to develop the topic.

❏ I used linking words, such as **another**, **for example**, and **also**, to connect ideas.

❏ I used precise language.

❏ I have a concluding statement.

Plan your response using this graphic organizer. Use your annotations and your notes on pages 68–73 to find text evidence for your essay.

Introduction:

Text Evidence:

Text Evidence:

Text Evidence:

Conclusion:

Wrap Up
Check Your Understanding

1. Which of the following statements would Thomas Jefferson most likely agree with?

    A. Ordinary words can accomplish extraordinary things.

    B. The British government had the right to control the American colonies.

    C. Ideas that are plain should be criticized and rewritten.

    D. The colonists complained too much about the British government.

2. What sentence best describes what Thomas Jefferson was trying to accomplish?

    A. Jefferson wanted to keep his grandchildren entertained.

    B. Jefferson wanted the delegates to stop arguing about his work.

    C. Jefferson wanted to help the British government keep its control of the colonies.

    D. Jefferson wanted to help the colonists break free of the British government.

3. What is the meaning of <u>masterly</u> as it is used in Jefferson's line in paragraph 11?

    A. committee

    B. honest

    C. expert

    D. youngest

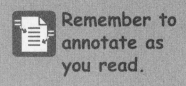
Notes

Thomas Jefferson *AND THE*
DECLARATION OF INDEPENDENCE

from the Monticello Classroom

1 In early May, 1776, Thomas Jefferson made a weeklong journey to Philadelphia to be a delegate to the Second Continental Congress. At thirty-three years old, he was the youngest member of Congress.

The Committee of Five

2 Congress appointed a committee of five to draw up a statement explaining why the colonies wanted independence. They chose John Adams of Massachusetts, Roger Sherman of Connecticut, Benjamin Franklin of Pennsylvania, Robert Livingston of New York, and Thomas Jefferson of Virginia.

3 Jefferson was thirty-three years old, one of the youngest members of Congress. He was not a fiery speaker. John Adams said of Jefferson, "During the whole time I sat with him in Congress, I never heard him utter three sentences together." Jefferson was known for his skill as a writer. The committee chose him to draft the declaration. Jefferson, however, wanted Adams to be the actual author. Adams reportedly replied, "You can write ten times better than I can."

Thomas Jefferson wrote the Declaration of Independence.

Drafting the Declaration of Independence

4   The committee met several times to talk about ideas and organization. Thomas Jefferson then set out to draft the declaration. He worked for two and a half weeks in the parlor of his rented rooms. He'd rise before dawn and have tea and biscuits. Quill pen in hand, he'd sit down at his "plain, neat, convenient" writing desk that he had designed. He ripped up early drafts. A small piece of an early draft remains, showing he changed nearly one-third of his words.

5   "I see my job as trying to bring together and harmonize a variety of different opinions," Jefferson wrote. "We are putting before all of mankind words that are both simple and firm, a justification for the stand that we're being forced to take."

Influences on Jefferson's Writing

6   Thomas Jefferson used no books or pamphlets to help him write the Declaration of Independence. Since his early days, he'd thought and read about government and the rights of mankind. He read British writer John Locke, who believed that people are born with natural rights. Governments should be for the benefit of everyone, not just the rulers. Thomas Paine had also expressed a similar idea in *Common Sense*: "A government of our own is a natural right."

Notes

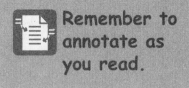

Notes

7   Jefferson's draft was also influenced by George Mason, a plantation owner in Virginia. Mason wrote a phrase similar to "pursuit of happiness" in his draft of "Virginia's Declaration of Rights." Jefferson was probably influenced by Dr. William Small of Scotland as well. Small had taught Jefferson for four years at the College of William and Mary. Jefferson described his professor as a man with "an enlarged and liberal mind."

8   "I did not consider it a part of my charge to invent new ideas," Thomas Jefferson later wrote about writing the Declaration, "but to place before mankind the common sense of the subject."

All Men are Created Equal

9   In the declaration, Jefferson linked many of these ideas. In the first part of the Declaration (called the preamble) he wrote that all men have rights, including "Life, Liberty and the pursuit of Happiness." He wrote that the colonies were no longer bound to England. Governments should get their power from the people, not a king.

This painting from 1819 shows the drafting of the Declaration of Independence.

10   In another section, Jefferson listed the many ways that King George III had neglected his duties to the people. These included "imposing taxes on us without our Consent" and "cutting off our Trade with all parts of the world."

11   Jefferson also drafted a section attacking the slave trade. He described slavery as "a cruel war against human nature itself, violating its most sacred rights of life and liberty."

12   The final draft was shown to Franklin and Adams. They made a few small changes before giving it to Congress on June 28th, 1776. However, delegates from South Carolina and Georgia would not sign it because of the language against slavery. There were also delegates from New England who would not sign because their merchants had profited from the slave trade. Congress debated the issue, and all language about slavery was taken out.

Independence!

13   From late Tuesday July 2 through Thursday July 4th, Congress made changes to Jefferson's draft of the Declaration. Jefferson's text was cut by about a fourth. Congress also included the words of Lee's Resolution "That these United Colonies are, and of Right ought to be Free and Independent States." On July 4th delegates from twelve colonies voted for the written declaration.

14   That day, in the late afternoon, Congress approved the written Declaration of Independence. John Hancock, president of Congress, signed it, making the document "legal and binding."

Notes

3 Independence

Remember to annotate as you read.

Notes

15   The first public reading of the Declaration of Independence was in Philadelphia on July 8th. The crowd cheered; church bells rang. By July 15th, all thirteen states had agreed to the resolutions in the new declaration.

16   The Declaration was written on parchment made from animal skin. On August 2nd, it was signed by the members of Congress, including Thomas Jefferson.

On July 8, 1776, the Declaration of Independence was read for the first time publicly on Independence Hall.

Impact of the Declaration of Independence

Notes

17   The Declaration of Independence is a famous document for many reasons. It declared the colonies' independence from Great Britain. It stated basic rights and liberties for Americans. The French used the ideals behind the Declaration as a model for their own revolution in 1789.

18   As time went by, the ideals behind "all men are created equal" grew in importance. Northern states used them to free slaves in their states. Abraham Lincoln used equal rights to justify the war against slavery. In 1963, Martin Luther King Jr. stood on the steps of the Lincoln Memorial in Washington, D.C. In his famous speech he repeated the ideals of the Declaration "that all men are created equal."

19   Women used equal rights to fight for the vote. In 1848, women at an equal rights meeting in New York wrote that "all men and women are created equal."

Women had to fight for equal rights. It took until 1920 before women could vote.

Close Reading and Collaborative Conversations

What Does the Text Say?	How Does the Text Work?
1. What is this text mostly about? Turn to a partner and summarize "Thomas Jefferson and the Declaration of Independence."	**1.** How are the accounts of the writing of the Declaration of Independence different in Passage 2 and Passage 3? How are they similar?
2. What are two main ideas of the "Influences on Jefferson's Writing" section?	**2.** What text structure does the author use to organize "Thomas Jefferson and the Declaration of Independence"?
3. Describe the impact of the Declaration of Independence.	**3.** What is the author's purpose for including the "Influences on Jefferson's Writing" section?

What Does the Text Mean?

1. What information from Passage 3 helps you better understand what you read in Passage 2? Use text evidence to support your answer.

2. How does the author support the point that Jefferson believed in equal rights for all?

3. How does the author of Passage 3 support the point that writing down your beliefs can empower others to overcome problems?

Write About the Text

Opinion/Argument Writing Prompt

Why do you think Thomas Jefferson was a good choice to write the first draft of the Declaration of Independence? Write an essay explaining your reasons. Give examples from the passage to support your opinion.

Writer's ✓Checklist

❑ I introduced the topic and clearly stated my opinion.

❑ I grouped related ideas together.

❑ I used facts to support my opinion.

❑ I used linking words, including **for example**, **because**, and **in addition**, to connect my ideas.

❑ I have a concluding statement.

Plan your essay using this graphic organizer. Use your annotations and your notes on pages 76–83 to find text evidence for your essay.

Introduction:	
Reason:	**Evidence:**
Reason:	**Evidence:**
Reason:	**Evidence:**
Conclusion:	

Wrap Up
Check Your Understanding

1. What central idea do Passage 1 and Passage 3 share?

   A. Thomas Jefferson faced a lot of difficulty and opposition when writing the Declaration of Independence.

   B. The French and Indian War was expensive and the British government taxed the American colonists to pay for it.

   C. The colonies fought a lot among themselves and the Declaration of Independence helped them come together.

   D. The British government tried to take away the American colonists' rights and freedoms, leading the colonies to break away from British rule and form their own government.

2. Which four statements belong in a summary of "Thomas Jefferson and the Declaration of Independence"?

   ☐ Thomas Jefferson's writing desk was plain, neat, and convenient.

   ☐ Thomas Paine and Thomas Jefferson shared similar ideas in their writing.

   ☐ Congress appointed a committee of five men to write a statement of why the colonies wanted independence.

   ☐ Thomas Jefferson was chosen to write the first draft of the Declaration of Independence.

   ☐ John Adams said that the whole time he sat with Thomas Jefferson, Jefferson never uttered three sentences together.

   ☐ Thomas Jefferson used the writing of others to help him write the first draft of the Declaration.

   ☐ The Declaration of Independence was written on parchment made from animal skin.

   ☐ The Declaration of Independence helped the American colonies break away from British rule.

 # Wrap Up

Check Your Understanding

3. This question has two parts. Answer Part A, then answer Part B.

Part A What is the meaning of <u>imposing</u> as it is used in paragraph 10?

A. taxing

B. forcing

C. spending

D. consenting

Part B Which phrase from the passage helps you understand the meaning of <u>imposing</u>?

A. "neglected his duties"

B. "cutting off"

C. "without our consent"

D. "life, liberty, and the pursuit of happiness"

4. The author states that Thomas Jefferson was probably influenced by his teacher, Dr. William Small. What sentence best supports this claim?

A. Dr. William Small taught at the College of William and Mary.

B. Jefferson described his professor as a man with "an enlarged and liberal mind."

C. Dr. William Small taught Thomas Jefferson for four years at the College of William and Mary.

D. Jefferson stated that he did not consider it part of his charge to invent new ideas.

Read and Write Across Texts

Plan your essay using this graphic organizer. Use your annotations and the notes you've taken on each passage to identify supporting evidence for your essay.

Introduction:

Evidence from "The French and Indian War Sets the Stage for the Revolution":

Opinion/Argument Writing Prompt

Jefferson wrote in the Declaration of Independence that all men have rights, including "life, liberty, and the pursuit of happiness." Write an essay explaining what these rights mean. Give examples from the passages to support your opinion.

③ Independence

Writer's ✓Checklist

❏ I introduced the topic and clearly stated my opinion.

❏ I grouped related ideas together.

❏ I used facts to support my opinion.

❏ I used linking words, including **for example**, **because**, and **in addition**, to connect my ideas.

❏ I have a concluding statement.

Evidence from "A Magical Pen":

Evidence from "Thomas Jefferson and the Declaration of Independence":

Conclusion:

Unit 4

Survival

Table of Contents

4 Survival

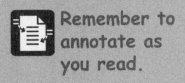
Notes

The Hodja and the Soup

1   A poor man had not eaten for two days so he went for a walk to try to forget his hunger, but his stomach would not let him forget. His tummy gurgled and made a loud noise that sounded like trumpets. Then his nose got a whiff of food cooking. "Ah," he said. "What a wonderful fragrance." It was fresh soup and the poor man could smell carrots, peppers, and tomatoes lingering in the air.

2   The poor man followed the smell to a restaurant with an opened window where he saw the pot of soup cooking on the stove. To the hungry man, it looked like heaven on Earth and smelled like pure joy. The man stood with his eyes closed and breathed in the good smell.

3   The restaurant owner rushed outside and asked the poor man what he was doing and the poor man told him that he was enjoying the smell of the soup. For some reason, this infuriated the restaurant owner, who told the poor man that he was not allowed to stand and sniff the soup. Then the owner grabbed him by the ear and dragged him inside the restaurant.

Accessing Complex Texts Now! • Grade 5 • ©2014 Benchmark Education Company, LLC

Notes

4   The owner told the poor man that in exchange for smelling the soup, he would have to wash dishes. Just then, Nasreddin Hodja came in for lunch. Known all over Turkey, Hodja was a wise teacher and a fair man. Hodja wanted to know what was going on.

5   The owner explained the situation and Hodja thought about the events. Then he said, "I will pay for this poor man."

6   The poor man's eyes lit up like two shooting stars and he began to thank Hodja profusely.

7   Then Hodja took out three coins and asked the restaurant owner if that was enough money to cover the smelling expense. The owner nodded and then Hodja dropped each coin onto the table. Plink, plink, plink, went the coins. Then Hodja scooped up the coins and put them back in his pocket.

8   The owner was confused and asked Hodja what he meant by that.

9   Hodja explained that the payment was just the sound of coins. The owner became furious again.

10   Hodja explained that it was not fair to expect a payment for smelling food, just as it wasn't fair to hear the sound of coins as payment. Then Hodja told the owner to go back to work and worry about people who would actually be eating at the restaurant.

11   Hodja then asked the poor man to lunch and they ate at a different restaurant where the owner did not charge for smelling the food.

4 Survival

Close Reading and Collaborative Conversations

What Does the Text Say?	How Does the Text Work?
1. What is this story about? Turn to a partner and summarize "The Hodja and the Soup."	**1.** From whose point of view is this story told? How does that influence the story?
2. Why does the restaurant owner not want the man smelling food outside his restaurant?	**2.** Why does the author say "the poor man's eyes lit up like two shooting stars"?
3. How does Hodja address the problem the restaurant owner presents to him?	**3.** What does the word "infuriated" mean as it is used in paragraph 3?

     Accessing Complex Texts Now! • Grade 5 • ©2014 Benchmark Education Company, LLC

What Does the Text Mean?

1. What lesson does the restaurant owner learn in the passage? Use details from the story to support your ideas.

2. What role does Hodja play in this story? How is Hodja similar to or different from other tricksters you have encountered in trickster tales?

3. How do the poor man's actions at the beginning of the story support the theme?

4 Survival

Write About the Text

Opinion/Argument Writing Prompt

How would the passage be different if it were written from the Hodja's point of view? Write a short essay explaining what information Hodja would include in the story. Use details from the passage to support your response.

Plan your response using this graphic organizer. Use your annotations and your notes on pages 90–93 to identify supporting evidence.

Introduction:

Text Evidence:

Text Evidence:

Text Evidence:

Conclusion:

Writer's ✓Checklist

❏ I introduced the topic and clearly stated my opinion.

❏ I grouped related ideas together.

❏ I used facts to support my opinion.

❏ I used linking words, such as **for example**, **because**, and **in addition**, to connect my ideas.

❏ I have a concluding statement.

# Wrap Up
Check Your Understanding

1. This question has two parts. Answer Part A, then answer Part B.

   Part A Why does Hodja decide to help the poor man?

      A. He is naturally kindhearted and intelligent.

      B. He wants to upset the restaurant owner.

      C. He was once poor himself.

      D. He does not like wealthy people.

   Part B Which statement from the passage gives the best support for the answer to Part A?

      A. "Just then, Nasreddin Hodja came in for lunch."

      B. "Known all over Turkey, Hodja was a wise teacher and a fair man."

      C. "The owner explained the situation and Hodja thought about the events."

      D. "Then Hodja took out three coins and asked the restaurant owner if that was enough money to cover the smelling expense."

2. How does the restaurant owner most likely feel at the end of the passage?

      A. upset

      B. proud

      C. guilty

      D. concerned

4 Survival

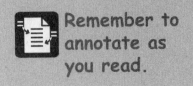
Notes

THREE GOLDEN APPLES
BY NATHANIEL HAWTHORNE

1   As Hercules came upon a giant, black clouds gathered about and burst into a tremendous storm, so that Hercules found it impossible to hear what the giant said.

2   At last, the storm swept over, and the giant roared out to Hercules anew.

3   "I am Atlas, the mightiest giant in the world! And I hold the sky upon my head!"

4   "So I see," answered Hercules. "But, can you show me the way to the garden of the Hesperides?"

5   "What do you want there?" asked the giant.

6   "I want three golden apples," shouted Hercules, "for my cousin, the king."

7   "There is nobody but myself," declared the giant, "to gather the golden apples. If it were not for this task of holding up the sky, I would make half a dozen steps across the sea, and get them for you."

8   "You are very kind," replied Hercules. "And cannot you rest the sky upon a mountain?"

9   "None of them are high enough," said Atlas. "But, if you were to stand on the summit, your head would be almost level with mine. What if you should take my burden on your shoulders, while I get the apples?"

10   "How long will it take to get the golden apples?"

11   "It will be done in a few moments," cried Atlas.

12   "Well, then," answered Hercules, "I will relieve you of your burden."

13   A little while later, the giant was back with apples in hand, and Hercules was glad to see him.

14   "It is a beautiful spot, that garden of the Hesperides. And the dragon with a hundred heads is a sight worth seeing."

15   "You have done the business as well as I could. I heartily thank you for your trouble. And now, as I have a long way to go, and am rather in haste—and as the king, my cousin, is anxious to receive the golden apples—will you be kind enough to take the sky off my shoulders again?"

16   "Why, as to that," said the giant, chucking the golden apples into the air twenty miles high, or thereabouts, and catching them as they came down, "as to that, I consider you unreasonable. Cannot I carry the golden apples to the king, your cousin, much quicker than you could? As His Majesty is in such a hurry to get them, I promise to take my longest strides."

Notes

4 Survival

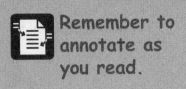
Notes

17   Hercules grew impatient and shrugged his shoulders, and a few stars tumbled out of place.

18   "Oh, that will never do!" cried Giant Atlas, laughing. "I have not let fall so many stars within the last five centuries. By the time you have stood there as long as I did, you will begin to learn patience!"

19   "Do you intend to make me bear this burden forever?" shouted Hercules.

20   "I bore it a good while longer, in spite of the backache. Well, then, after a thousand years, if I happen to feel in the mood, we may possibly shift about again. You are certainly a very strong man, and can never have a better opportunity to prove it."

21   "Incredibly unfair!" cried Hercules, with another hitch of his shoulders. "Just take the sky upon your head one instant, will you? I want to make a cushion of my lion's skin, for the weight to rest upon. It really chafes me, and will cause unnecessary inconvenience in so many centuries as I am to stand here."

22   "That's no more than fair, and I'll do it!" declared the giant, for he had no unkind feelings towards Hercules, and was merely acting with a too selfish consideration of his own ease. "For just five minutes, then, I'll take back the sky."

23   Ah, the thick-witted old rogue of a giant! He threw down the golden apples, and received back the sky, from the head and shoulders of Hercules. And Hercules picked up the three golden apples, that were as big or bigger than pumpkins, and straightaway set out on his journey homeward, without paying the slightest heed to the thundering tones of the giant, who bellowed after him to come back.

24　　And there stands the giant to this day; or at any rate, there stands a mountain as tall as he, and which bears his name; and when the thunder rumbles about its summit we may imagine it to be the voice of Giant Atlas, bellowing after Hercules!

Notes

Close Reading and Collaborative Conversations

What Does the Text Say?	How Does the Text Work?
1. What is this story about? Turn to a partner and summarize "Three Golden Apples."	**1.** What is the narrator's point of view about the giant? Use details from the text to support your answer.
2. What does the passage tell you about the giant's personality?	**2.** What is the tone of this story? Use details from the text to support your answer.
3. How is Hercules's personality different from that of the giant?	**3.** What is the author's purpose in paragraph 24?

What Does the Text Mean?

1. What lesson does Atlas learn in this passage? Use details from the text to support your answer.

2. How is this myth similar to other myths you have read? How is it different? Use evidence from the text to support your response.

3. Compare the characters Hodja and Hercules. How are the two characters similar? How are they different? Use details from the text to support your answer.

4 Survival

 Write About the Text

Writer's Checklist

- ❑ I introduced the topic and clearly stated my opinion.
- ❑ I grouped related ideas together.
- ❑ I used facts to support my opinion.
- ❑ I used linking words, such as **for example**, **because**, and **in addition**, to connect my ideas.
- ❑ I have a concluding statement.

Plan your response using this graphic organizer. Use your annotations and your notes on pages 96–101 to identify supporting evidence.

Introduction:

Text Evidence:

Text Evidence:

Text Evidence:

Conclusion:

Wrap Up
Check Your Understanding

1. This question has two parts. Answer Part A, then answer Part B.

Part A What is most likely Hercules's attitude toward the giant in the middle of the story?

    A. He feels scared and mystified by him.

    B. He feels warmth and concern for the giant's problems.

    C. He feels frustrated and annoyed by him.

    D. He feels angry and vengeful toward him.

Part B Which statement from the passage provides the best support for the answer to Part A?

    A. "'You are very kind,' replied Hercules."

    B. "'Do you intend to make me bear this burden forever?' shouted Hercules."

    C. "Ah, the thick-witted old rogue of a giant!"

    D. "He threw down the golden apples, and received back the sky, from the head and shoulders of Hercules."

2. In paragraph 23 of the passage, what is the meaning of the word <u>heed</u>?

    A. attention

    B. respect

    C. friendship

    D. effort

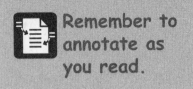

Remember to annotate as you read.

Notes

Bushi's Bullfight

retold by Phillis Gershator

1   "The Emperor of Japan sent me a gift, a magnificent bull," announced Sho Ko, king of Okinawa. "And you, Matsumura, my chief bodyguard, will fight this beast!"

2   Matsumura had no wish to fight a bull, but it was not his place to question the king. Still, the question, *Why?* must have been revealed in his eyes, for the king continued to speak, raising his voice a notch, as though a loud voice were more convincing than a soft one.

3   "Our annual festival is about to begin. I will entertain my subjects with noise and spectacle, and they will forget their grievances, their talk of poverty and taxes. And they will have the pleasure of witnessing the famous and powerful Matsumura crush a beast with his bare hands, just as he would crush my enemies."

4   Hoping to avert the king's proposed fight, Matsumura said, "I may not be quite that powerful, Your Highness."

Notes

5   The king, in the manner of a stubborn bull, charged ahead. "Crush the beast or go to prison. That is your choice."

6   Sokon Matsumura had been trained in Te, the martial arts of his birthplace, and had become its acknowledged master. He might be able to kill the bull before it killed him; but even so, the fight itself was cruel and unnecessary. A true warrior did not engage in violence for the sake of violence. A true warrior promoted discipline, peace, prosperity, and virtue.

7   Matsumura left the palace, observing the world around him with renewed appreciation. *If I were locked away in a deep, dark dungeon*, he thought, *I'd never see my friends and family again . . . never see the trees, lakes, mountains . . . never see the flowers blooming in their appointed seasons. . . .* He sighed deeply as he bent down to inhale the perfume of a blossom—then jumped back with a start, clapping his hand over his stinging nose.

8   "Ouch! A bee!"

9   Once the pain subsided, he laughed at himself. "I will never again close my eyes to smell a flower. I've learned my lesson! And from such a tiny teacher, too. My teacher must have studied Master Sun's Art of War," he said, rubbing his swollen nose.

10   "Attack when there is no defense."

11   As he said those words, a thought struck him. The king offered a choice: Crush the beast or go to prison. But there was another way—the way of the true warrior!

12   Matsumura had one day to teach the lessons he'd learned. Arriving at the king's stables, he announced, "I wish to meet my adversary for tomorrow."

4 Survival

Notes

13   "At your service," replied the stable keeper, leading the way to the bull's pen.

14   The bull was indeed magnificent, a sleek hulking creature, all thick bones and heavy muscles, and black as night. It weighed more than a ton and stood more than six feet—taller than Matsumura, who was himself a tall man.

15   The bull tossed its huge head and pawed the ground with its mighty hoofs. At Matsumura's request, the stable keeper tied the bull with ropes so it could not move.

16   Then Matsumura stepped inside the pen. He took a fighting stance and addressed the bound bull. "Great horned one, I am not your enemy. I do not want to kill you—it is not the way of the warrior to do something so unnatural. For this reason, I fervently hope you will learn the lesson I am about to teach you."

17   With a rush of air, Matsumura emitted a shout that sent crows flying from the treetops. "HYAH!" At the same time, he lunged forward, pricking the bull's soft nose with a long, sharp pin.

18   The bull bellowed in pain and anger, straining against the ropes. Matsumura waited quietly until the bull calmed down. Then, once again standing as though ready to strike, he let loose a shout from deep within, a sound so intense it sent rats scurrying into their holes. Even the bull winced at the sound! "HYAH!"

19   Matsumura again lunged forward to prick the bull's nose, and again the bull struggled and bellowed in frustration.

20   Matsumura repeated his "lesson" a third time. "HYAH!" The poor bull could not escape the sharp pin, the pain, the ropes, or the gaze of those two determined, deep-set eyes.

21   *He is a madman, as mad as our king!* thought the stable keeper. *He will surely die tomorrow! An enraged bull against an unarmed madman—no contest!*

22   Okinawans from every town and village converged on Shuri, the royal capital, to enjoy the festivities— banners waving, drums beating, food frying, fireworks exploding—and, of course, the sword contests, martial arts exhibitions, and bullfights.

23   Bulls fought each other at the king's festival, butting heads and locking horns, until one bull either fell to its knees or ran away from its opponent. But never before had a bare-handed man fought a bull. How could even the best martial artist in the land defend himself against such a huge and ferocious beast?

24   Matsumura was the only person not enjoying the festivities. He couldn't allow himself to be tempted by distractions—not even a bowl of his favorite yakisoba noodles. He concentrated on clearing his mind, breathing deeply in and out, expelling every worldly thought and feeling. When he calmly entered the arena, he was free from hope and fear, focused and relaxed—ready for the fight.

Notes

4 Survival

Remember to annotate as you read.

Notes

25   The bull was ready, too. It barged through the gates the moment they were opened, snorting menacingly. The massive beast lowered its head and charged the man in the center of the ring.

26   Matsumura shifted to one side to avoid the charging bull. "HYAH!" he shouted, his cry echoing like a roll of thunder. The bull paused, recognizing the sound and scent of the man with the long, sharp pin. The bull's nose quivered.

27   Man and bull stood head to head. The crowd was silent. The man will surely be gored and trampled now. What a tragedy!

28   Then the bull turned and ran—in the opposite direction!

29   Matsumura followed the bull. He shouted again, "HYAH!"

30   The bull had learned the lesson it was meant to learn: Stay away from the man with the pin! Evading its pursuer, the bull escaped through the open gates, back into the safety of its pen.

31   Matsumura sighed with relief. Master Sun was right. "What discourages an opponent is the prospect of harm." He bowed to the king and to the cheering crowd.

32   The crowd roared. "Bushi, bushi! Warrior, warrior!"

33   The king promptly made a speech.

34   "Matsumura is so powerful, even the emperor of Japan's raging bull is afraid of him. Matsumura is a great warrior, and Bushi—Warrior! will now be his name."

35   Sokon "Bushi" Matsumura, the king's chief bodyguard, saved the life of an innocent bull—and lived the rest of his own long life as a free man. When King Sho Ko was forced to leave his throne, Bushi served as chief bodyguard for the two kings who succeeded him: King Sho Iku and King Sho Tai, the last king of Okinawa. Bushi's own grandson and grandson's nephew, along with Bushi's spiritual descendants, carried on his teachings, taught today throughout the world wherever martial artists seek the way of the true warrior.

Notes

Close Reading and Collaborative Conversations

What Does the Text Say?	How Does the Text Work?
1. What is this story about? Turn to a partner and summarize "Bushi's Bullfight."	**1.** Reread paragraphs 14 and 15. What does the reader learn from the description of the bull?
2. What problem does Matsumura have in the beginning of the story?	**2.** Why are paragraphs 7 and 8 important to the story?
3. Describe the character of the king in this story.	**3.** Who is the narrator in this story? How does it affect how the story is told?

What Does the Text Mean?

1. What the theme of this story? Use evidence from the text to support your response.

2. Based on what you read in the story, what is a true warrior? What are examples of how a true warrior would behave?

3. Compare the characters Hodja, Hercules, and Bushi. How are these characters similar? How are they different? Use details from the text to support your response.

Write About the Text

Informative/ Explanatory Writing Prompt

What is Bushi's point of view about fighting the bull? After reading "Bushi's Bullfight," write two paragraphs explaining Bushi's views. Use details from the text to support your response.

Writer's Checklist

❏ I introduced the topic.

❏ I used facts and examples to develop the topic.

❏ I used linking words, such as **another**, **for example**, and **also**, to connect ideas.

❏ I used precise language.

❏ I have a concluding statement.

Plan your response using this graphic organizer. Use your annotations and your notes on pages 104–111 to identify supporting evidence.

Introduction:

Text Evidence:

Text Evidence:

Text Evidence:

Conclusion:

Wrap Up
Check Your Understanding

1. If the bull could be said to have a point of view, how does it change during the passage?

   A. At first it hates Bushi, but then it comes to be friends with him.

   B. In the beginning, it is scared of Bushi, but then it grows more relaxed around him.

   C. The bull is angry at the start of the passage but then views the fight as a kind of game.

   D. It is ready to kill Bushi at the passage's beginning, but then learns to stay away.

2. This question has two parts. Answer Part A, then answer Part B.

   Part A What can you infer about the king from the passage?

   A. He is a wise and strong ruler.

   B. He is tough and cruel.

   C. He is compassionate toward humans and animals.

   D. He is more interested in his own goals than others'.

   Part B Which sentence from the passage best supports the answer to Part A?

   A. "'And you, Matsumura, my chief bodyguard, will fight this beast!'"

   B. "'Our annual festival is about to begin.'"

   C. "I will entertain my subjects with noise and spectacle, and they will forget their grievances, their talk of poverty and taxes."

   D. "'Crush the beast or go to prison.'"

Wrap Up
Check Your Understanding

3. What was the gift that the Emperor sent to King Sho Ko?

    A. a nice letter

    B. a magnificent bull

    C. Matsumura

    D. a special grandson

4. What did Sokon "Bushi" Matsumura gain by saving the bull's life?

    A. He went to prison.

    B. He lived the rest of his life as a free man.

    C. He carried on his teachings.

    D. He was given free food.

Read and Write Across Texts

Plan your essay using this graphic organizer. Use your annotations and the notes you've taken on each passage to identify supporting evidence for your essay.

Introduction:

Evidence from "The Hodja and the Soup":

Opinion/Argument Writing Prompt

Which of the three main characters in this unit is the most admirable? Write an essay comparing the characters and explaining which one you think is most admirable and why. Use details from the text to support your ideas.

Writer's Checklist

- ❑ I introduced the topic and clearly stated my opinion.
- ❑ I grouped related ideas together.
- ❑ I used facts to support my opinion.
- ❑ I used linking words, such as **for example**, **because**, and **in addition**, to connect my ideas.
- ❑ I have a concluding statement.

4 Survival

Evidence from "Three Golden Apples":

Evidence from "Bushi's Bullfight":

Conclusion:

Unit 5
Exploration

Table of Contents

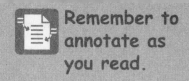

Remember to annotate as you read.

Notes

SACAGAWEA

1   Imagine yourself a teenager, just 16 or 17 years old. Could you lead visitors through your old neighborhood, a place you had last seen as a child of 11 or 12? Could you also care for your spouse and newborn baby? Sacagawea, the only woman to travel with Lewis and Clark, did this and more.

2   In 1804, Sacagawea was living among the Mandan and Hidatsa. That is near present-day Bismarck, North Dakota. Just four years earlier, she had been kidnapped from her home in Idaho. She was taken from her people, the Lemhi Shoshone. Living among the Mandan and Hidatsa, Sacagawea married French trader, Toussaint Charbonneau. In February 1805, she gave birth to a baby boy. It was her first child.

Sacagawea joined the Lewis and Clark Expedition in 1805.

3   Two months after the birth of her son, Sacagawea left the Mandan and Hidatsa villages to journey west with the Lewis and Clark Expedition. While Sacagawea is often remembered as the guide who led the group across the plains, Expedition journals don't offer much evidence of this. Historians generally believe that Sacagawea joined the Expedition because her husband had been hired as a translator. Still, Sacagawea contributed significantly to the success of the journey.

4   Sacagawea helped because she was a woman. Among the tribes the explorers met, her presence dispelled the notion that the group was a war party. William Clark explained that "the Wife of Shabono [Charbonneau] . . . reconciles all the Indians, as to our friendly intentions. A woman with a party of men is a token of peace."

5   Once the group reached Idaho, Sacagawea's knowledge of the landscape and the Shoshone language came in handy. The explorers were eager to find the Shoshone and trade with them for horses. The success of the journey hinged on finding the tribe. Without horses, the explorers would be unable to get their supplies over the mountains. Recognizing landmarks in her old neighborhood, Sacagawea reassured the explorers that the Shoshone and their horses were close. When the Expedition did meet the Shoshone, Sacagawea helped the men communicate. She helped translate along with her husband.

6   As the explorers traveled eastward in 1806, returning to St. Louis, they stopped again at the Mandan and Hidatsa villages. There, Sacagawea and her family ended their journey.

Notes

Exploration

Close Reading and Collaborative Conversations

What Does the Text Say?	How Does the Text Work?
1. What is the main idea of this passage? Turn to a partner and summarize "Sacagawea."	**1.** Reread paragraph 1. What is the author's purpose in this paragraph?
2. Why was Sacagawea's work on the Expedition so difficult? Provide evidence from the text.	**2.** What is the overall structure of the passage? Use details from the text to support your answer.
3. Why did Sacagawea join Lewis and Clark? Why was her help needed?	**3.** Reread paragraph 4. Why does the author include the quote from Clark? Why is it important to the passage?

What Does the Text Mean?

1. Does the author give enough evidence to show that Sacagawea was helpful on the journey? Why or why not? Use evidence from the text to support your answer.

2. The text states that Lewis and Clark needed a translator on their journey. What inferences can you make based on that fact?

3. What inferences can you make about the Lewis and Clark Expedition after reading this passage? Use details from the passage to support your ideas.

5 Exploration

Write About the Text

Informative/ Explanatory Writing Prompt

After reading "Sacagawea," write an essay that summarizes Sacagawea's contributions to the Lewis and Clark Expedition. Support your discussion with evidence from the text.

Writer's ✓Checklist

❏ I introduced the topic.

❏ I used facts and examples to develop the topic.

❏ I used linking words, such as **for example**, **also**, and **because**, to connect ideas.

❏ I used precise language.

❏ I have a concluding statement.

Plan your response using this graphic organizer. Use your annotations and your notes on pages 118–121 to identify supporting evidence.

Introduction:

Example:

Supporting Text Evidence:

Example:

Supporting Text Evidence:

Conclusion:

# Wrap Up
Check Your Understanding

1. Which explanation best describes what William Clark means as <u>token of peace</u> in Paragraph 4?

   A. symbol of peace

   B. money for peace

   C. piece of forgiveness

   D. written treaty or agreement

2. This question has two parts. Answer Part A, then answer Part B.

   Part A What is the author's purpose for writing "Sacagawea"?

   A. to entertain the reader with a story about a Shoshone princess

   B. to inform the reader about the accomplishments of Sacagawea

   C. to inform the reader about details of the Lewis and Clark Expedition

   D. to persuade the reader to learn more about Sacagawea

   Part B Which sentence from the passage supports the answer to Part A?

   A. "Expedition journals don't offer much evidence of this."

   B. "Imagine yourself a teenager, just 16 or 17 years old."

   C. "As the explorers traveled eastward in 1806, returning to St. Louis, they stopped again at the Mandan and Hidatsa villages."

   D. "Sacagawea, the only woman to travel with Lewis and Clark, did this and more."

5 Exploration

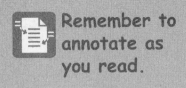
Remember to annotate as you read.

Notes

The Louisiana Purchase

Most of the land the United States purchased was unexplored wilderness.

1 It has been called the greatest real estate deal in history! On April 30, 1803, France sold 828,000 square miles of land west of the Mississippi River to the United States. This has become known as the Louisiana Purchase.

2 The Louisiana Purchase was the largest and most extraordinary land purchase in the history of the United States. It doubled the size of the country. It was also the cheapest. The final cost, at $15 million, was less than five cents per acre.

3 The land stretched from the Mississippi River to the beginning of the Rocky Mountains. Present states that were included in part or whole were Arkansas, Colorado, Iowa, Kansas, Minnesota, Missouri, Montana, Nebraska, New Mexico, North Dakota, Oklahoma, South Dakota, Texas, and Wyoming. Much of it was unexplored wilderness.

Notes

4   Americans had been moving farther westward from the time of the first colonies. By the late 1700s, explorers and pioneers had crossed the Appalachian Mountains and headed for parts known and unknown. Pioneer Daniel Boone arrived in what is today the state of Kentucky in 1767 and spent 30 years exploring the area. Boone and other pioneers blazed trails and roads into the frontier, allowing more settlers to follow. They were looking for better farmland and more land for livestock. Soon, the land west of the Appalachian Mountains to the Mississippi River was bustling with Americans. The Mississippi River had become an important way to transport goods. The river and the port of New Orleans were vital to Americans living on the frontier.

5   The Louisiana Purchase started with an offer to purchase New Orleans and the surrounding area. The United States government wanted to protect America's access to the river and the port. They didn't want another country to have control over it.

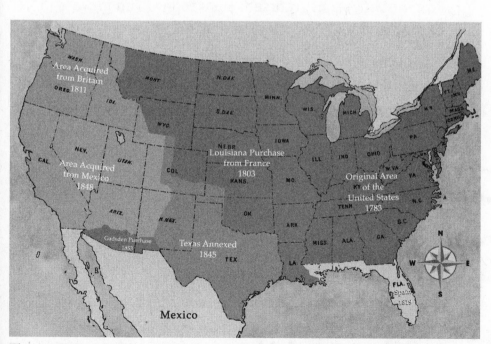

The Louisiana Purchase greatly increased the size of the country.

Remember to annotate as you read.

Notes

New Orleans was an important port. Jefferson wanted to protect America's access to it.

6   President Thomas Jefferson sent Robert Livingston to France with an offer to buy New Orleans and the surrounding area. Napoleon, who was by this time Emperor of France, refused. He was involved in wars in Europe and had dreams of a western empire as well.

7   After his initial refusal, Jefferson sent James Monroe to France, in hopes of convincing Napoleon to reconsider. The French leader did more than that. He offered to sell all of the Louisiana Territory. That's because things were going badly for him and he needed the money.

8   As President of the United States, Thomas Jefferson faced opposition to the purchase of the land. Some people said that it was unconstitutional and undermined the authority of the states in the government. The U.S. Constitution didn't have any provisions for acquiring territory, so Jefferson was exploring new bounds of governmental control.

9   But Jefferson felt strongly that he didn't want France and Spain to have the ability to cut off the United States' access to the Mississippi River and the port of New Orleans. The purchase was announced on July 4, 1803. The Senate approved the Louisiana Purchase Treaty in October and the United States took possession of the territory in December 1804.

10   In one simple transaction, the country doubled in size. The American government made a down payment on the land in gold totaling $3 million. The rest was financed in bonds by some of the most important banks in Europe at the time. Then France cashed the bonds to use the money to pay off debts.

11   The purchase of the land would open up the continent to westward expansion. Even before the purchase was finalized, President Jefferson arranged for two men, Meriwether Lewis and William Clark, to lead an expedition across the continent to explore the land.

Today, the nickel commemorates President Jefferson and the Louisiana Purchase.

Notes

Exploration

5

Close Reading and Collaborative Conversations

What Does the Text Say?	How Does the Text Work?
1. What is the big idea the author wants you to know in this passage? Turn to a partner and summarize "The Louisiana Purchase."	**1.** How does the map help the reader understand the passage better? What additional information does it provide?
2. Why did France's emperor, Napoleon, refuse Jefferson's first offer to buy the land surrounding New Orleans?	**2.** What is the text structure of paragraph 8? Provide evidence to support your answer.
3. What did the Louisiana Purchase include? Provide evidence from the passage to support your answer.	**3.** What does it mean that the U.S. Constitution did not have "provisions for acquiring territory"? What details in the text help you understand the meaning?

What Does the Text Mean?

1. What does the author mean by the first sentence of the article: "It has been called the greatest real estate deal in history"? Use details from the text to support your answer.

2. Why was the Louisiana Purchase an important event in American history? Use text evidence from the passage to support your answer.

3. How does this passage help you better understand the first passage? What important background information does it provide?

Write About the Text

Informative/ Explanatory Writing Prompt

After reading "The Louisiana Purchase," write an essay that explains the events that lead to the Louisiana Purchase, including Jefferson's motivations. Support your ideas with evidence from the text.

Writer's ✓ Checklist

❏ I introduced the topic.

❏ I used facts and examples to develop the topic.

❏ I used linking words, such as **for example**, **also**, and **because**, to connect ideas.

❏ I used precise language.

❏ I have a concluding statement.

Plan your response using this graphic organizer. Use your annotations and your notes on pages 124–129 to identify supporting evidence.

The first event: Details: • • •	Another event: Details: • • •

Topic Sentence:

Another event: Details: • • •	Conclusion:

# Wrap Up
Check Your Understanding

1. What reasons did some Americans give for opposing the Louisiana Purchase? Choose all that apply.

☐ It undermined state governments.

☐ It undermined the federal government.

☐ It was unconstitutional.

☐ It blocked access to important ports.

☐ It was unapproved by the Senate.

2. This question has two parts. Answer Part A, then answer Part B.

Part A Why was controlling the port of New Orleans important to Thomas Jefferson?

A. It was close to important farmland.

B. It kept the French out of the United States.

C. It helped the government receive shipments from France.

D. It helped Americans transport goods along the Mississippi.

Part B Which sentence from the passage supports the answer to Part A?

A. "They were looking for better farmland and more land for livestock."

B. "The American government made a down payment on the land in gold totaling $3 million."

C. "The purchase was announced on July 4, 1803."

D. "The United States government wanted to protect America's access to the river and the port."

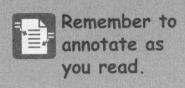

Notes

THE EXPEDITION *of* Lewis AND Clark

1   In 1804, Meriwether Lewis and William Clark led an expedition to explore the territory west of the Mississippi River. The land had become part of the United States with the Louisiana Purchase. Lewis and Clark were friends who also happened to know President Thomas Jefferson. (Lewis was, in fact, Jefferson's private secretary at the time.)

2   The Lewis and Clark Expedition is more than the story of two men; it is the story of many individuals and groups, and it included military men and scientists, a president and a slave, women and men, French-speaking boatmen and Native Americans. The team was known as the Corps of Discovery.

3   Thomas Jefferson wanted Lewis and Clark to provide a clear picture of the West, so the men on the Expedition were to observe and record everything, from Native American languages to the dates when plants flower. In fulfilling Jefferson's request, the explorers became amateur scientists. They kept detailed journals, and gathered examples of hundreds of new species of plants and animals.

For the first part of the journey, the Corps of Discovery traveled by boat up the Missouri River. They traveled an average of 10 to 15 miles a day.

Notes

Sacagawea and her husband, Charbonneau, traveled with Lewis and Clark and acted as translators.

4   Both Lewis and Clark had served in the army and were familiar with exploring and with Native Americans. They were not, however, familiar with the territory they were about to see.

5   Relying on their skills as soldiers and leaders, they planned to take a team of about thirty on the journey. They would travel from the Missouri Territory to the source of the Columbia River. During the winter of 1803–1804, Lewis and Clark assembled their team. Among them were fourteen other soldiers; nine frontiersmen from Kentucky; two French boatmen; and Clark's servant, York.

6   On May 14, 1804, the Expedition officially began. The teams sailed up the Missouri River from a point near St. Louis. They stopped from time to time, and reached the Dakota Territory near wintertime, where they decided to build a fort and stay for the winter.

7   While in the Dakota Territory, they met a French man named Toussaint Charbonneau, who offered to guide them on their journey. Charbonneau also brought along his Shoshone wife, Sacagawea, as a guide. The Expedition resumed in the spring. While samples of the local wildlife and plantlife made their way back to Thomas Jefferson in Washington, D.C., Lewis and Clark and their team set out west.

⑤ Exploration

Notes

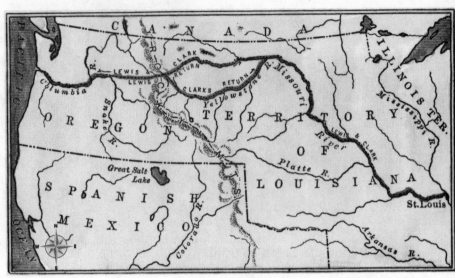

This map shows Lewis and Clark's route. President Jefferson wanted Lewis and Clark to look for a water route to the Pacific Ocean while they were exploring the new territory.

8   They followed the Missouri River west until they reached the Great Falls. Here, the water was too rough and they had to carry their canoes around the falls. Despite this back breaking one-month delay, they pressed on.

9   Soon, they were in Shoshone territory. Sacagawea's language skills came in handy. Communication between Lewis and Clark and the Shoshone proved difficult but not impossible. Sacagawea would listen to what her fellow Shoshone were saying. Then she would tell her husband what they said in Hidatsa, another Native American language. Charbonneau, who also spoke Hidatsa, would translate into French. He would tell expedition member François Labiche, who would translate into English for the team leaders.

10   Lewis and Clark had also discovered that Sacagawea knew much about the territory they were all traveling through. She knew the safe paths over mountains and down rivers. She knew where her family lived, and where they could get fresh horses and supplies.

Notes

11   When Lewis wanted the Shoshone to know that he and his men came in peace, he offered gifts and used sign language, a few Shoshone words, and red paint (the Shoshone color for peace) to tell them.

12   Although the Shoshone welcomed Lewis, they were suspicious. They had been raided by another tribe. When Lewis asked them to travel to meet the rest of the Expedition party, the Shoshone wondered if they were being trapped. It was Sacagawea who helped smooth things out between Lewis and the Shoshone. It helped that her brother was the chief. Crossing the Continental Divide proved difficult, even in warm weather. Snow was still on some of the paths. But by September, the Corps of Discovery was on the other side of the Rocky Mountains and traveling onward. In fact, they had left the land behind.

13   They reached the Clearwater River, which would take them to the Columbia River and, eventually, to the Pacific Ocean. And on November 7, 1805, they saw the great ocean. They celebrated their achievement and built a fort. It was there that they spent the winter.

Lewis and Clark reached the Pacific Ocean on November 7, 1805.

Remember to annotate as you read.

Notes

14   The next March, they started on the trip home. A few months later, Lewis and Clark split up, in order to cover more territory. Clark and several men went southeast to the Yellowstone River, and followed it to the Missouri. Lewis took Sacagawea and several men and went northeast. As on the trip west, they kept detailed notes and gathered samples of unfamiliar animal and plant life.

15   On Lewis's part of the journey home, he was involved in a skirmish with Native Americans. (This was the only fight of the entire journey, in both directions.) Lewis's bad luck continued several days later when one of his own men accidentally shot him while they were out hunting. The party eventually made it to the Dakota Territory, where Lewis recovered and they left Sacagawea and her family. Incredibly, she had given birth to a baby just before they had departed the Dakota Territory, in 1804, and had carried that baby on her back during the entire expedition. When she arrived home, the baby was two years old.

16   Here also, Lewis and Clark hooked up again and headed back to St. Louis. They arrived there on September 22, 1806. In the more than two years of their journey, they had covered 8,000 miles and discovered 173 new plants and 122 species and subspecies of animals.

Lewis and Clark took detailed notes about the wildlife in their journals.

The Journals of Lewis and Clark

17   **For more than 200 years, the Expedition journals have been a source of knowledge and understanding. Here are some entries from the journals of Lewis and Clark:**

18   *It rained during the greater part of last night and continued until 7 o'clock A.M., after which the party proceeded. The barge ran foul there several times on logs, and in one instance it was with much difficulty they could get her off. Happily no injury was sustained, though the barge was several minutes in imminent danger. This was caused by her being too heavily laden in the stern. Persons accustomed to the navigation of the Missouri, and the Mississippi also, below the mouth of this river, uniformly take the precaution to load their vessels heaviest in the bow when they ascend the stream, in order to avoid the danger incident to running foul of the concealed timber, which lies in great quantities in the beds of these rivers.*
—Captain Lewis, 15 May 1804

19   *We passed a creek twelve yards wide, on the L.S. [left side], coming out of an extensive prairie reaching within two hundred yards of the river. As this creek has no name, and this being the Fourth of July, the day of the Independence of the United States, we called it "Fourth of July 1804 Creek." We dined on corn. Captain Lewis walked on shore above this creek and discovered a high mound from the top of which he had an extensive view. Three paths came together at the mound. We saw great numbers of goslings today which were nearly grown. The lake is clear and contains great quantities of fish and geese and goslings. This induced me to call it Gosling Lake. A small creek and several springs run into the lake on the east side from the hills. The land on that side is very good.*
—Captain Clark, 4 July 1804

Notes

_____

_____

_____

_____

_____

_____

_____

_____

_____

_____

_____

_____

_____

_____

_____

_____

_____

_____

_____

_____

5 Exploration

Close Reading and Collaborative Conversations

What Does the Text Say?	How Does the Text Work?
1. What is this passage mostly about? Turn to a partner and summarize "The Expedition of Lewis and Clark."	**1.** How is the text organized? Give an example from the text to support your answer.
2. Why did the Corps of Discovery take notes about the plant and animal life they saw? Use evidence from the text to support your answer.	**2.** What information can readers learn from the firsthand accounts in Lewis and Clark's journals that they can't learn from the passage?
3. How long did it take for Lewis and Clark to reach the Pacific Ocean? How long did the entire expedition take?	**3.** What information is included in the map that is not included in the passage? How does it help the reader?

What Does the Text Mean?

1. Why was the Lewis and Clark Expedition important? Use evidence from all three passages to support your ideas.

2. The author states that the Lewis and Clark Expedition is "the story of many individuals and groups." What details does the author use to support this statement?

3. Compare the information about Sacagawea in Passage 1 with the information in Passage 2. What additional information did you learn from this passage?

⑤ Exploration

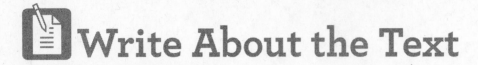

Write About the Text

Writer's Checklist

❏ I introduced the topic.

❏ I used facts and examples to develop the topic.

❏ I used linking words, such as **for example**, **also**, and **because**, to connect ideas.

❏ I used precise language.

❏ I have a concluding statement.

Plan your response using this graphic organizer. Use your annotations and your notes on pages 132–139 to identify supporting evidence.

Introduction:

Text Evidence:

Text Evidence:

Text Evidence:

Conclusion:

# Wrap Up
Check Your Understanding

1. Which choices below are events that occurred during the Lewis and Clark Expedition? Choose the events and number them in the correct order.

   ___ The corps made a fort near the Dakota Territory to spend the winter.

   ___ The corps reached the Atlantic Ocean.

   ___ The corps joined with Toussaint Charbonneau and his wife, Sacagawea.

   ___ The team stayed with the Shoshone tribe for several years.

   ___ The team met and communicated with the Shoshone Native Americans.

   ___ A team of explorers was put together.

   ___ The team sailed up the Missouri River from the St. Louis area.

2. This question has two parts. Answer Part A, then answer Part B.

   Part A Why did Meriwether Lewis offer the Shoshone red paint?

   A. to show that he was ready to battle

   B. to show that he came in peace

   C. to ask for help and directions

   D. to offer help to the Shoshone

   Part B Which phrase from the passage supports the answer to Part A?

   A. "translate into English for the team leaders"

   B. "fresh horses and supplies"

   C. "the Shoshone color for peace"

   D. "used sign language"

 Wrap Up
Check Your Understanding

3. Which words best describe the explorers in the Corps of Discovery?
Choose all that apply.

☐ soldiers

☐ educated

☐ leaders

☐ brave

☐ unprepared

☐ peaceful

4. Why were the Shoshone suspicious of the Expedition?

A. They had never seen settlers before.

B. They had been raided by another tribe.

C. They could not understand Sacagawea.

D. They knew they were going to be trapped.

Read and Write Across Texts

Plan your essay using this graphic organizer.
Use your annotations and the notes you've taken on each
passage to identify supporting evidence for your essay.

Introduction:

Evidence from "Sacagawea":

Writer's Checklist

❏ I introduced the topic and clearly stated my opinion.

❏ I grouped related ideas together.

❏ I used facts to support my opinion.

❏ I used linking words, such as **for example**, **because**, and **in addition**, to connect my ideas.

❏ I have a concluding statement.

5 Exploration

Evidence from "The Louisiana Purchase":

Evidence from "The Expedition of Lewis and Clark":

Conclusion:

Unit 6
Hurricanes

Table of Contents

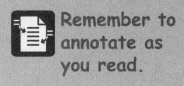
Notes

Flying Through a Hurricane

Robbie Hood (right) is a scientist who studies hurricanes.

1   Most people's eyes would be glued to the window—or tightly shut—when flying through a hurricane. Instead, Robbie Hood stares mostly at her computer monitor.

2   Hood is an atmospheric scientist at NASA's Marshall Space Flight Center in Huntsville, Alabama. She has flown several times into the fury of the whirling storms. She claims it's not as scary as it sounds.

3   "The view out of the aircraft windows can be somewhat boring," said Hood. "The aircraft is often flying through clouds so there is not much to see."

4   There is plenty to look at on her laptop, however. It displays a stream of atmospheric data being collected by the instruments and sensors outside the aircraft. The goal is to use the data to improve understanding and prediction of hurricanes.

Excerpted from NASA's Earth's Explorers

Notes

5   But why send an airplane into the middle of a hurricane when there are satellites that can make observations from space? Hood says that the aircraft data, when combined with satellite information, gives scientists a more detailed view of how hurricanes work. Measurements taken from inside the storm are also used to check the accuracy of the satellite data.

6   "We're putting the storm under a microscope," said Hood. "You can see the storm structures in higher detail (than from satellites alone)."

7   Hood's fascination with weather and hurricanes goes back to her days growing up in the South. Raised on a cattle farm in Missouri, she became very familiar with the impact weather can have on agriculture. Hood's family also happened to be in Mississippi when Hurricane Camille slammed into the Gulf Coast.

8   "To see the kind of damage that it could do made a big impression on me," said Hood. She remembers the storm knocking out power, downing trees, and blowing the roofs off of houses.

9   Their severity is not the only thing that sparks Hood's interest in hurricanes. She is also attracted by the human qualities assigned to the storms. In fact, Hood has always been a bit of a people person.

10   "I credit my Native American heritage with my interest and appreciation of people," said Hood. She is a member of the western tribe of the Cherokee nation. "I think I like studying hurricanes because they act so much like people. Hurricanes have names and personalities and don't behave like we expect them to sometimes."

6 Hurricanes

Close Reading and Collaborative Conversations

What Does the Text Say?	How Does the Text Work?
1. What is this passage mostly about? Turn to a partner and summarize "Flying Through a Hurricane."	**1.** Reread paragraph 1. What is the author's purpose in this paragraph?
2. How do scientists use planes to understand hurricanes?	**2.** Why does the author include information about Hood's childhood? Why is the information important?
3. What are two effects of collecting hurricane data in an aircraft? Provide evidence from the text.	**3.** How do the quotes from Hood help the reader understand the text?

What Does the Text Mean?

1. Hood says that hurricanes are like people. What inferences can the reader make about hurricanes from her description and the information in the text?

2. What does Hood mean when she says, "We're putting the storm under a microscope"? What details in the text support this idea?

3. Why is the work that Robbie Hood does important? What evidence does the author use to support this idea?

Write About the Text

After reading "Flying Through a Hurricane," write an essay explaining the reasons why scientists fly through hurricanes. Support your discussion with evidence from the text.

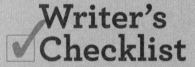 ## Writer's Checklist

❏ I introduced the topic.

❏ I used facts and examples to develop the topic.

❏ I used linking words, such as **another**, **for example**, and **also**, to connect ideas.

❏ I have a concluding statement.

Plan your essay using this graphic organizer. Use annotations and your notes on pages 146–149 to identify text evidence.

Introduction:

Text Evidence:

Text Evidence:

Text Evidence:

Conclusion:

 # Wrap Up
Check Your Understanding

1. This question has two parts. Answer Part A, then answer Part B.

   Part A What is the author's purpose for writing "Flying Through a Hurricane"?

   A. to entertain the reader with a story about storms

   B. to inform the reader about how hurricanes form

   C. to inform the reader about ways people study hurricanes

   D. to persuade the reader to learn more about how hurricanes form

   Part B Which text from the article supports the answer to Part A?

   A. "The goal is to use the data to improve understanding and prediction of hurricanes."

   B. "She is a member of the western tribe of the Cherokee nation."

   C. "She remembers the storm knocking out power, downing trees, and blowing the roofs off of houses."

   D. "Measurements taken from inside the storm are also used to check the accuracy of the satellite data."

2. Which of the following inferences can you make from the passage? Check the box next to each correct answer.

   ☐ Scientists need to use many tools and methods to predict hurricanes.

   ☐ All atmospheric scientists do research from planes.

   ☐ Scientists have to gather a lot of data to understand hurricanes.

   ☐ Robbie Hood spends all of her time in a plane.

   ☐ Satellites are the most important tool for studying hurricanes.

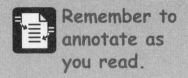

Notes

What They Saw

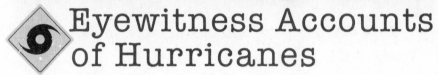

Eyewitness Accounts of Hurricanes

1   If you are a hurricane survivor, chances are you remember the date and details of the event. For many people, surviving a hurricane can be a life-altering experience. These are eyewitness accounts of people who have lived through a hurricane.

Hurricane Andrew, 1992

2   **Hurricane Andrew hit the coastline of southern Florida on August 24, 1992. It was a Category 5 hurricane. The wind speeds were over 160 miles per hour.**

3   "Within seconds, we actually heard Hurricane Andrew bearing down on us. It slammed into us with all the force of a speeding locomotive. The horrendous wall of winds crashed against our tiny apartment like an exploding bomb! Glasses flew off the kitchen counter, shattering onto the quaking floor. Hanging pictures plunged straight down the walls toward the ground. The huge hanging mirror crashed on top of the television set. It sprayed the living room with shattered glass. The entire apartment resembled a rickety old train that was shaking fiercely out of control while rumbling down a railroad track. The screeching winds quickly transformed into the piercing, monotone hum of a jet engine. It sounded as if it had sucked us up inside! It was so deafening. All other noises ceased to exist. It felt like a monstrous earthquake and tornado hitting at the same time!

4   "Before either of us could react, the metal front door of our apartment began to peel steadily downward toward the floor, like a piece of wet, limp paper. Then the voracious jaws of Andrew attacked for a final kill. A mega-giant two-story-tall solid concrete transformer pole with electrical cables attached, torpedoed through our living room wall and roof. The building exploded on impact. And that was just the beginning.

5   "Hurricane Andrew had shifted course. The monstrous storm packing sustaining winds of 175 mph, with gusts expected higher, was not coming over Broward County, as first forecasted by the National Hurricane Bureau. Now it was Dade County that was under emergency alert. All South Dade residents were advised to seek shelter immediately. Our apartment was not much bigger than a double-width trailer. It had been constructed to safely withstand 90 mph winds but anything exceeding that was unsafe. At that precise moment I felt as though I were trapped in a plane flying thirty thousand feet above ground, and the captain had just informed us that the wings had fallen off. Swallowing hard, I tried to steady my voice in a whisper, 'Move the piano up against the front door. Come on. We haven't got much time.'"

Hurricane Andrew was one of the most expensive disasters in U.S. history.

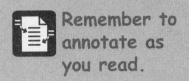
Notes

Flooding during a hurricane can be severe.

Hurricane Audrey, 1957

6 **Hurricane Audrey hit the coast of southern Louisiana and southeastern Texas on June 27, 1957.**

7 "We stayed upstairs and I stood for hours at the head of the steps and watched the water coming up closer and closer to the top stairs. The wind was blowing about 125 miles per hour. It made huge waves of water splash upstairs in the hall. Huge logs, animals, and snakes came in and washed on through.

8 "When it was light enough to see the downstairs hall, we saw a tree lodged against the stairs. The floor was deep in mud. The water and debris had rushed in through the large front opening and out through the back doors and windows, which had all disappeared. This river flowing through the house kept the water from rising to the second floor. After an hour or so, I ventured downstairs. The first thing I saw in one of the rooms was a snake coiled on an old mattress. I turned around and ran back upstairs."

Hurricane Camille, 1969

9 **Hurricane Camille made landfall in Mississippi on August 17, 1969.**

10 "I could not believe what I saw! The barrier islands had not been able to stop the waves that came with the hurricane. The water had risen to twenty feet above the normal level. Everything in the path of the hurricane was either blown apart or flooded, or both. The strong winds and the high waves killed 143 people and did billions of dollars in damage. Our little beach house was completely gone, along with all of our furniture and clothing. There was no electricity for several days. The water was unsafe to drink. But then everyone worked together to help rebuild the community."

Notes

Buildings along the shore face the greatest risks during a hurricane.

Hurricanes

Close Reading and Collaborative Conversations

What Does the Text Say?	How Does the Text Work?
1. What is this passage mostly about? Turn to a partner and summarize "What They Saw."	**1.** How does the introduction to each hurricane help the reader better understand the eyewitness account that follows?
2. What do each of these descriptions have in common?	**2.** How does the description of water in the second and third accounts help the reader understand the dangers of hurricanes?
3. What kind of damage can severe hurricanes do? Provide evidence from each account to support your answer.	**3.** In the first account, what figurative language is used to describe Hurricane Andrew? Give two examples from the text.

What Does the Text Mean?

1. What do the eyewitness accounts help the reader understand about hurricanes? What information does the reader get from a firsthand account that they don't get from a secondhand account?

2. Why does the author say that hurricanes can be a "life-altering experience" for some people? Use details from the text to support your answer.

3. Reread the account of Hurricane Andrew. What role did the hurricane forecasting play during Andrew?

Write About the Text

Opinion/Argument Writing Prompt

After reading "What They Saw: Eyewitness Accounts of Hurricanes," write an essay in which you choose which of the three accounts is most effective and explain why. Support your reason with evidence from the text.

Plan your essay using this graphic organizer. Use annotations and your notes on pages 152–157 to identify which account you found most effective and why.

The first reason:	Another reason:
Details:	Details:
•	•
•	•
•	•

Topic Sentence:

Another reason:	Conclusion:
Details:	
•	
•	
•	

Writer's Checklist

☐ I introduced the topic and clearly stated my opinion.

☐ I grouped related ideas together.

☐ I used facts to support my argument.

☐ I used linking words, such as **for instance, in order to, in addition,** to connect my ideas.

☐ I have a concluding statement.

 # Wrap Up

Check Your Understanding

1. What does the author mean by the phrase <u>eyewitness account</u>?

   A. retelling of a recent event

   B. retelling of an important event in history

   C. explanation by someone who was at an event

   D. explanation by someone who heard about an event

2. Which phrase from the eyewitness account of Hurricane Andrew is used to describe the hurricane's winds?

   A. "a piece of wet, limp paper"

   B. "a monstrous earthquake"

   C. "a rickety old train"

   D. "the monotone hum of a jet engine"

3. Which of the following words describes the feelings of the person who gave the eyewitness account of Hurricane Audrey in 1957? Select all the answers that apply.

   ☐ cautious

   ☐ fearful

   ☐ impatient

   ☐ amused

   ☐ disgusted

Hurricanes

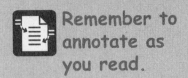

Remember to annotate as you read.

Notes

HURRICANES:
The Greatest Storms on Earth

1   There are few things in nature that compare to the destructive force of a hurricane. Hurricanes are called the greatest storms on Earth because a hurricane can wipe out coastal areas with heavy winds, intense rainfall, and storm surges.

2   The term *hurricane* comes from Huracan. He was the god of evil recognized by the Tainos, an ancient aboriginal tribe from Central America. In other parts of the world, hurricanes are known by other names. In the western Pacific and China Sea area, hurricanes are known as typhoons, from the Cantonese *tai-fung*, meaning "great wind." In Bangladesh, Pakistan, India, and Australia, they are known as *cyclones*, and finally, in the Philippines, they are known as *bagyo*.

3   The scientific term for all these storms is *tropical cyclone*. Only tropical cyclones that form over the Atlantic Ocean or eastern Pacific Ocean are called *hurricanes*.

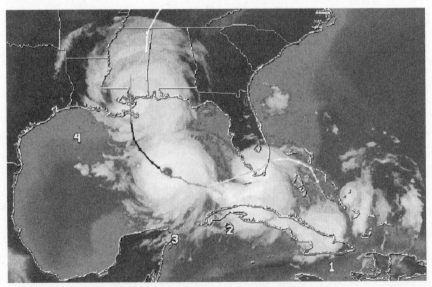

This satellite image shows the path of Hurricane Katrina, which hit the coast of Louisiana and Mississippi in 2005.

Adapted from NASA Space Place

The winds from a hurricane can tear the roofs off houses.

Notes

How Hurricanes Form

4   Whatever they are called, tropical cyclones all form the same way. Tropical cyclones are like giant engines that use warm, moist air as fuel. That is why they form only over warm ocean waters near the equator. The warm, moist air over the ocean rises upward from the surface. When the warm air rises, it causes an area of low pressure below.

5   Air from surrounding areas with higher air pressure pushes in to the low-pressure area. Then that "new" air becomes warm and moist and rises, too. As the warm air continues to rise, the surrounding air swirls in to take its place. As the warmed, moist air rises and cools off, the water in the air forms clouds. The whole system of clouds and wind spins and grows, fed by the ocean's heat and water evaporating from the surface.

6 Hurricanes

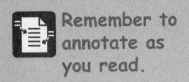
Notes

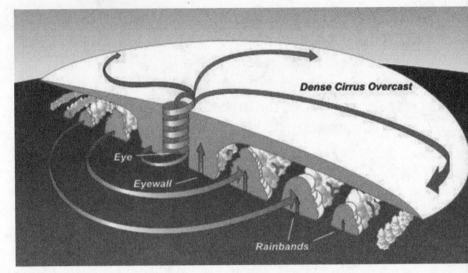

Dense Cirrus Overcast

Eye

Eyewall

Rainbands

This cross-section of a hurricane shows how the bands of rain circulate around an eye.

6   As the storm system rotates faster and faster, an eye forms in the center. It is very calm and clear in the eye, with very low air pressure. Higher pressure air from above flows down into the eye.

7   When the winds in the rotating storm reach 39 mph, the storm is called a *tropical storm*. And when the wind speeds reach 74 mph, the storm is officially a *tropical cyclone*, or hurricane.

8   Tropical cyclones usually weaken when they hit land. That's because they are no longer being "fed" by the energy from the warm ocean waters. However, they often move far inland. They can dump many inches of rain and cause lots of wind damage before they die.

9   In the early 1970s, a classification system was designed to measure the level of damage and flooding expected from a hurricane. This system was invented by Herbert Saffir, an engineer, and Robert Simpson, then the director of the National Hurricane Center. It is called the Saffir-Simpson Hurricane Intensity Scale. It consists of five categories. One is the weakest and five is the strongest. The scale corresponds to a hurricane's central pressure, sustained winds, and storm surge.

10   The number of hurricanes that occur annually vary from ocean to ocean. The most active area is the western Pacific Ocean. It contains a wide expanse of warm ocean water. In contrast, the Atlantic Ocean averages about ten storms annually, of which six reach hurricane status.

11   During a hurricane, homes, businesses, roads, and bridges may be damaged or destroyed by high winds and high waves. Debris from the high winds can damage property. Roads and bridges can be washed away by flash flooding or can be blocked by debris. In particularly large storms, the force of the wind alone can cause tremendous devastation. Trees and power lines topple and weak homes and buildings crumble. These losses are not just limited to the coastline. Damage can often extend hundreds of miles inland.

Notes

Even Category 1 hurricanes have the power to bring down trees.

6 Hurricanes

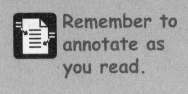
Notes

12   When hurricanes hit land, they bring with them multiple hazards, including storm surges, winds, tornadoes, and inland flooding.

13   **Storm Surges** This mass of water from the ocean is pushed onto land by the hurricane. The storm surge is the greatest threat to life and property along the immediate coast.

14   **Winds** Hurricane-force winds, 74 mph or more, can destroy buildings and mobile homes. Debris, such as signs, roofing material, siding, and small items left outside, become flying missiles in hurricanes. Winds can stay above hurricane strength well inland. Hurricane Hugo (1989) battered Charlotte, North Carolina—about 175 miles inland—with gusts to near 100 mph, downing trees and power lines.

Notes

15   **Tornadoes** Hurricanes and tropical storms can also produce tornadoes. Usually, tornadoes produced by hurricanes are relatively weak and short-lived, but they still pose a threat.

16   **Inland Flooding** All tropical cyclones can produce heavy rains. The rains can be more than six inches. This rain can produce deadly and destructive floods. Flooding is the major threat from tropical cyclones to people who live inland, or away from the coast. Flash flooding, a rapid rise in water levels, can occur quickly due to intense rainfall. Rivers and streams inland can cause flooding several days after the storm.

For people living on the coast, the storm surge is one of the biggest dangers from a hurricane.

⑥ Hurricanes

Close Reading and Collaborative Conversations

What Does the Text Say?	How Does the Text Work?
1. What are the big ideas in this passage? Turn to a partner and identify what you think are two big ideas.	**1.** How is the text organized? Give an example from the text to support your answer.
2. Why is it useful to have a scale for measuring the intensity of a hurricane? Use evidence from the text to support your answer.	**2.** How does the cross-section of a hurricane on page 160 help the reader understand hurricanes?
3. What conditions are needed for a hurricane to form?	**3.** What is the author's purpose for writing this article?

What Does the Text Mean?

1. Based on what your have read in all three passages, why is it important for scientists to understand hurricanes?

2. The passage states that hurricanes can also be dangerous for people living inland. What evidence does the author provide to support that idea?

3. What does the text say is the most damaging part of a hurricane? Use evidence from the text to support your opinion.

Ⓖ Hurricanes

Write About the Text

After reading "Hurricanes: The Greatest Storms on Earth," write an essay in which you explain what happens when a hurricane hits land. Use details from the text to support your ideas.

Writer's ✓ Checklist

❏ I introduced the topic.

❏ I used facts and examples to develop the topic.

❏ I used linking words, such as **another**, **for example**, and **also**, to connect ideas.

❏ I used precise language.

❏ I have a concluding statement.

Plan your essay using this graphic organizer. Use annotations and your notes on pages 160–167 to identify text evidence.

Introduction:

Text Evidence:

Text Evidence:

Text Evidence:

Conclusion:

☑ Wrap Up
Check Your Understanding

1. Which conditions are needed for a hurricane to form? Choose the conditions and number them in the correct order.

   ___ A center, or eye, forms with rotating air speeding up around it.

   ___ Warm air over land in cool areas.

   ___ Warm air over warm oceans.

   ___ A high-pressure system moves to the west.

   ___ System of spinning clouds growing faster, fed by hot air below.

   ___ Storm clouds rotate until they reach land, then stop suddenly.

   ___ Air rises and low-pressure air below it warms.

2. This question has two parts. Answer Part A, then answer Part B.

   Part A What does the author mean by the word <u>fed</u> in paragraph 8?

   A. to change slightly

   B. to grow quickly

   C. to be given food

   D. to be kept moving

   Part B Which sentence from the passage helps you understand the answer to Part A?

   A. "That 'new' air becomes warm and moist and rises, too."

   B. "When the warm air rises, it causes an area of low pressure below."

   C. "Tropical cyclones are like giant engines that use warm, moist air as fuel."

   D. "It is very calm and clear in the eye, with very low air pressure."

⑥ Hurricanes

 Wrap Up

Check Your Understanding

3. What is the biggest problem hurricanes cause once they reach inland areas?

    A. flying debris

    B. flooding

    C. storm surge

    D. heavy winds

4. Which of the following is necessary for the formation of a tropical cyclone?

    A. warm moist air

    B. the Atlantic Ocean

    C. winds over 74 mph

    D. ocean water

Read and Write Across Texts

Plan your essay using this graphic organizer.
Use your annotations and the notes you've taken on each
passage to identify supporting evidence for your essay.

Introduction:

Evidence from "Flying Through a Hurricane":

Writer's Checklist

- ❏ I introduced the topic and clearly stated my opinion.

- ❏ I grouped related ideas together.

- ❏ I used facts to support my argument.

- ❏ I used linking words, including **for instance, in order to, in addition,** to connect my ideas.

- ❏ I have a concluding statement.

6 Hurricanes

Evidence from "What They Saw":

Evidence from "Hurricanes: The Greatest Storms on Earth":

Conclusion:

Notes

Notes

Notes

Acknowledgments

"Narcissa" from *Bronzeville Boys and Girls*, ©1956, 1984 by Gwendolyn Brooks. Used by permission of HarperCollins Publishers.

"A Different Drummer" reprinted by permission of Carus Publishing Company, 30 Grove Street, Suite C, Peterborough, NH 03458 from *Cricket* magazine, February 2013, Vol. 40, No. 5, text © 2013 by Diana C. Conway. All rights reserved. www.cricketmag.com.

"Foul Ball," reprinted by permission of Carus Publishing Company, 30 Grove Street, Suite C, Peterborough, NH 03458 from *Cricket* Magazine, February 2013, Vol. 40, No. 5, © 2013 Carus Publishing Company. www.cricketmag.com.

"Oceans of Grass," by Kathleen Weidner Zoehfeld, *Ask* Magazine, February 2013, © 2013 Carus Publishing Company, published by Cobblestone Publishing, 30 Grove Street, Suite C, Peterborough, NH 03458. www.caruspub.net.

"The French and Indian War Set the Stage for the Revolution" from the National Park Service, http://www.nps.gov/fone/forteachers/classrooms/fi-unit6.htm.

"A Magical Pen," by Ruth Spencer Johnson, from *Appleseeds* issue: Thomas Jefferson, © 2006 Cobblestone Publishing Company, 30 Grove Street, Suite C, Peterborough, NH 03458. All Rights Reserved. Used by permission of the publisher. www.cobblestonepub.com.

"Jefferson and the Declaration of Independence" from The Monticello Classroom, © 2007 Thomas Jefferson Foundation. classroom.monticello.org.

"Bushi's Bullfight" reprinted by permission by Carus Publishing Company, 30 Grove Street, Suite C, Peterborough, NH 03458 from *Cricket* magazine, March 2013, Vol. 40, No. 6, text © 2013 by Phillis Gershator. All rights reserved. www.cricketmag.com.

"Sacagawea" from National Park Service. http://www.nps.gov/lecl/historyculture/sacagawea.htm.

"The Expedition of Lewis and Clark" adapted from the U.S. National Archives and Record Service. http://www.archives.gov/education/lessons/lewis-clark.

"Flying Through a Hurricane with Robbie Hood" http://pmm.nasa.gov/education/articles/flying-through-hurricanes-robbie-hood.

"What They Saw" from NOAA History, A Science Odyssey and from Multicultural Education Through Miniatures, http://www.coedu.usf.edu/culture/story/story_mississippi.htm.

"Hurricanes: The Greatest Storms on Earth" adapted from NASA Earth Observatory. http://earthobservatory.nasa.gov/Features/Hurricanes.

Photo Credits:

Page 42, 43: NOAA; Page 70: © Bettmann/Corbis; Page 80, 123: © North Wind/North Wind Picture Archives; Page 81, 115, 116, 124, 130, 131, 134: The Granger Collection, NYC; Page 122: © Niday Picture Library/Alamy; Page 132: © North Wind Picture Archives/Alamy; Page 133: © George Ostertag/Alamy; Page 143: © Naval Atlantic Meteorology and Oceanography Center/Corbis; Page 144B: Chris Sattlberger/Science Source; Page 158, 159, 160: Chris Sattlberger/Science Source; Page 162: MIKE THEISS/National Geographic Creative.

Illustration Credits

Narcissa Ayesha Lopez
A Different Drummer Naomi Hocking
Three Golden Apples Ovi Hondru
Bushi's Bullfight Yishan Li